MEDITATIONS IN
Matthew

# MEDITATIONS IN
Matthew

A Daily Devotional

STEPHEN MANLEY

Beacon Hill Press of Kansas City
Kansas City, Missouri

Copyright 1992
by Beacon Hill Press of Kansas City

ISBN: 083-411-4275

Printed in the
United States of America

Cover Design: Crandall Vail

All Scripture quotations beginning each day's devotionals are from *The Holy Bible, New International Version* (NIV), copyright © 1973, 1978, 1984 by the International Bible Society, and are used by permission of Zondervan Bible Publishers.

All quotations in the main body of the text are from the *New King James Version* (NKJV), copyright © 1979, 1980, 1982, Thomas Nelson, Inc., Publishers, and are used by permission.

Dedication

My ability to grasp the spiritual truths contained in this book come as a result of the personal sacrifices of a very special lady. She gladly bore physical pain in my birth, lovingly cared for me in childhood, willingly worked to pay for my college education, and has consistently surrounded me with the expression of her own love, which brings meaning and purpose to my life. My encounter with her has not been a brief, temporary involvement; it has been for a lifetime. I dedicate this book to Edwinna Manley, my mother.

Acknowledgments

I wish to express sincere gratitude to Mary Lou Fisher, a faithful secretary in the midst of my intensity, and to Carol Wight Gritton for her excellent editorial work.

Introduction

Matthew was an evangelist. He desperately wanted to convert the Jews to Christianity. His convincing message is contained in his account of the Gospel. Its focus is a presentation of Jesus Christ as the Kingly Messiah. Every paragraph of every chapter is pointing to the authority of this Kingly Messiah. It ranges from miracles to conquering sin, from delivering demon-possessed individuals to speaking a healing word, and from fulfilling the purpose for which He came to bring life out of death.

After the opening devotional, we begin our daily investigation in Matthew 8. It is an action chapter. Jesus has come from the preaching scene where He delivered the great principles of the kingdom of God. Now those principles are going to be lived out in vivid life situations. The strength of this study is in the day-after-day investigation. There is repetition, but it is on purpose. We are using the personal Bible study technique of "saturation." We are allowing our lives to settle into these verses day after day until God can speak to us. Don't rush through them. Don't fall into the trap of thinking you have covered this material before. Live in the passage.

• MATTHEW 7:28-29 •

Mark 1:22

"The people were amazed at his teaching, because he taught them as one who had authority, not at the teachers of the law."

HEART OF THE MATTER

Each of the writers of the New Testament had a distinct purpose in writing. Matthew, in his Gospel, is writing to the Jews to convince them that Jesus is the Kingly Messiah. His strong argument: "authority."

After Jesus had finished the great Sermon on the Mount, Matthew reflects on His preaching records: "He taught them as one having authority" (Matt. 7:29).

The people had been astonished with Jesus' speaking. He had given insight into the Old Testament as no one had ever done before. Not only was the law presented, but Jesus, the heart of the law, had been seen. He had a right to speak the truth to them.

There are a lot of voices crying for our attention; some are within and some without. But there is only One who has the right to speak directly to us. His authority is clearly established in who He is and what He has accomplished.

Prayer

"Jesus, I place my life in Your hands as an act of belief in Your authority. Teach me the heart of truth."

• MATTHEW 8:1-4 •

Ps. 95:6-7

"Come, let us bow down in worship, let us kneel before the Lord our Maker; for he is our God and we are . . . under his care."

WORSHIP IS "WORTH IT"

One of the first encounters of Jesus as recorded in Matthew's Gospel is with a leper. Interaction with a leper in Christ's day was extreme. It was certainly a strong testing of the loving words of the Sermon on the Mount.

In describing the incident, Matthew said, "And behold, a leper came and worshiped Him" (8:2).

Worship gets the immediate attention of Jesus. Worship becomes the avenue that allows the flow of divine life from Him to us. In the middle of programs, activities, and performances it is important to worship.

"Worship," meaning "worth it," is the expression of the inner heart saying to Jesus, "You are worth it." It is a pledge of loyalty and love, a life-style as well as an experience. As we take some moments for concentrated worship, we find it will be worth it, because He is.

Prayer

"Jesus, I bring all that I am and bow in worship before You, my Lord and God, not only in my quiet moments but also with the activity of my life."

• MATTHEW 8:1-4 •

Jer. 29:11
"For I know the plans I have for you . . . plans to prosper you and not to harm you, plans to give you hope and a future."

GOOD AND WILLING

"Lord, if You are willing, You can make me clean," the leper said to Jesus (Matt. 8:2).

"I am willing," responded Jesus. "Be cleansed" (v. 3).

There are those who cling to these verses to prove that Jesus is always willing to heal. Yet many continue to bear illness in spite of prayer and belief. There is one thing that can be derived from these words, and that is Jesus' willingness to bring the best to our lives.

The truth is, it is not always best to give us our own way. There are unknown factors that we are incapable of piecing together. Because of this, we must have total faith in the love of Christ. We must believe that He is good, and that He knows what is good for us.

We can trust Him with our whole life because He has never done anything but good for us.

Prayer

"Jesus, even in the presence of turmoil, I rest in the confidence of Your love, which plans the best for me."

• MATTHEW 8:14-15 •

Heb. 9:14
"How much more, then, will the blood of Christ, who through the eternal Spirit offered himself unblemished to God, cleanse our consciences . . . so that we may serve the living God!"

HEALED TO SERVE

Jesus had gone to Peter's home in Capernaum (Matt. 8:14-15), where Peter's mother-in-law was sick with a fever. It was a simple matter for Jesus to touch her hand and remove the fever. But the revealing thing about this story is that the woman immediately rose and served them. She was healed to serve.

James, in his Epistle, talks to us about the motivation behind our prayers. There seems to be a block to receiving answers because we ask with improper motive. We desire to use answered prayer for our own selfish reasons, and it becomes destructive (4:2-3). We are healed, not just to be healed, but to serve.

When service results, it continues the process of healing by passing it along to a wounded world.

Prayer

"Jesus, as I consider my healings, I make myself available to pass along the blessing received, through service to others."

• MATTHEW 8:18-22 •

Matt. 10:39

"Whoever finds his life will lose it, and whoever loses his life for my sake will find it."

LIFE ON THE LEVEL

Today, when one hears the call to discipleship from Christ, it is the same as in the days of the New Testament.

A scribe, who had been thrilled with the preaching and miracles of Jesus, gave a token surrender to Christ. But Jesus warned him, "Foxes have holes and birds of the air have nests, but the Son of Man has nowhere to lay His head" (Matt. 8:20).

For one who was interested in the easy time that a health-and-wealth Messiah could offer, this was startling news. It was a call to replace materialism with a desire for eternal values. It would demand that we place the needs of others ahead of our own. It would require aligning our will with the will of God.

All in all, discipleship is not too attractive unless one wants life on the level of Christ. But isn't that what we need?

Prayer

"Jesus, help me to continually evaluate and adjust daily activities so that they stay on the level of a 'life of surrendered discipleship.'"

• MATTHEW 8:18-22 •

Luke 14:27

"And anyone who does not carry his cross and follow me cannot be my disciple."

TEMPORARY PRIDE— EXTERNAL COMFORT

A disciple of Jesus requested that he be allowed to postpone following Christ until he had buried his father. Is this unreasonable (Matt. 8:21)? It is, if we understand that his father wasn't dead. The request was made out of pride, lest the family name be hindered without the eldest son present to conduct the family affairs.

Our pride allows pressure from the outside world to shape our inward soul. Our pride listens to the pressure of this temporal world in regard to building that which is eternal.

One method of clearing up the confusion is to listen to the voice of Christ. He cuts through our pride with the sharp edge of His Word and calls us to total commitment in a world that exerts its pressures.

His voice rings with the authority of the One who is Lord. Listen closely!

Prayer

"Jesus, speak to me above the loud clatter of my life and the voices of others. I want to hear Your voice above all the rest."

• MATTHEW 8:23-27 •

Rom. 8:38-39

"Neither death nor life, neither angels nor demons, neither the present nor the future, nor any powers, neither height nor depth, nor anything else in all creation, will be able to separate us from the love of God that is in Christ Jesus our Lord."

IN THE BOAT

In Matt. 8:23-27, Jesus and His disciples are in a ship going across the sea. "A great tempest arose on the sea, so that the boat was covered with the waves" (v. 24).

The disciples were afraid. One might consider that to be a normal reaction. But, remember what the disciples had experienced just a few hours earlier. They had seen Jesus perform miracles, and He was sitting in their boat. They had seen the wonders of His touch, but, still, they were afraid.

We come to church to sing praises, but we easily forget what we have experienced when a new crisis arises.

Jesus is the Answer to the storms of life. And He is sitting beside us in the boat.

Prayer

"Jesus, fill me so much with Your presence that even in the darkest night I can see the light of Your face."

• MATTHEW 8:23-27 •

Ps. 62:1-2

"My soul finds rest in God alone; my salvation comes from him. He alone is my rock and my salvation; he is my fortress, I will never be shaken."

REST THROUGH THE STORM

In the middle of the storm, wouldn't it be great to fall asleep and awaken to find the storm gone?

Life isn't like that. It wasn't ever that way for Jesus. The disciples and He were on their way across the sea when the waves became so strong they covered the boat (Matt. 8:24). The disciples were afraid. But Jesus was asleep in the storm.

We can identify with the disciples. Who could sleep at a time like that? We may have forgotten that the ability to rest in the storm is the result of an inner condition; rest and relaxation are products of inner peace, not outward conditions. One must be right within.

This doesn't mean the storms will go away. The ability to *deal* with the storms of life comes from the rest in the soul. And such rest comes from the confidence of His power within.

Prayer

"Jesus, I rest my life in Your power to bring peace to the furious waves."

• MATTHEW 9:9-10 •

Ps. 139:23-24

"Search me, O God, and know my heart; test me and know my anxious thoughts. See if there is any offensive way in me, and lead me in the way everlasting."

COMPARED TO JESUS

Matthew was a tax collector and not what you would call socially acceptable.

He was a Jew who had betrayed his own people by joining forces with Rome. He had bought this tax collecting job to further his financial gain, and he did so by taxing the people whatever he wanted. He paid Rome what they required and pocketed the rest. It's no wonder everyone hated him.

We would place Matthew right up front as a sinner with a capital S. We are usually quite content to find someone worse than we are and, in comparison, we look all right. But when we do this, we overlook our own need—the weaknesses, the faults, and the flaws—which should be brought to Jesus.

Prayer

"Jesus, I bring myself to You so that I can see 'me' clearly in the light of Your mercy and accept others in the light of Your love."

Matt. 9:9

"Jesus . . . saw a man named Matthew sitting at the tax collector's booth. 'Follow me,' he told him, and Matthew got up and followed him."

THE EYES OF GOD

Jesus touches, loves, and embraces those who are not acceptable to others. We see this in the conversion of Matthew, a sinner and publican (9:9-10).

The biblical account says that Jesus "saw a man named Matthew." Others who had looked in Matthew's direction did not see a man, but love cleared the atmosphere and made it possible to see.

Jesus also saw with eternal perspective and "said to him, 'Follow Me!'"

If we see people through the clear atmosphere of love, we will no doubt be able to call them to something better. Something beyond the temporary, to something—Someone—eternal.

We need to remember when looking at others that Jesus called us when He saw us through His clear eyes of love.

Prayer

"Jesus, help me refocus daily so that I see others through Your eyes."

• MATTHEW 9:11-13 •

Matt. 9:12-13

"It is not the healthy who need a doctor, but the sick. . . . For I have not come to call the righteous, but sinners."

HIS BODY

One of the most important questions ever asked concerning Christ is, "Why does your Teacher eat with tax collectors and 'sinners'?" (Matt. 9:11).

The Pharisees could not understand a Messiah rubbing shoulders with "those kind" of people. But Jesus gave them new insight when He said, "Those who are well have no need of a physician, but those who are sick" (v. 12).

Can you imagine a physician who does not want to get near the sick? Can you comprehend a cook who does not want to be in the kitchen? Can you visualize a lover who does not want to be with his beloved?

Jesus, a Messiah whose desire is to be where there is need, has decided to fill us with His Spirit, using our flesh as His body to meet the need.

Prayer

"Jesus, show me today who needs Your touch through my hands."

• MATTHEW 9:14-17 •

Matt. 16:24
"If anyone would come after me, he must deny himself and take up his cross and follow me."

RADICAL LIVING

There was quite a contrast between the disciples of Christ and the Pharisees. The followers of John the Baptist, noticing this, asked, "Why do we and the Pharisees fast often, but Your disciples do not fast?" (Matt. 9:14) Jesus, in answering, spoke of a bridegroom.

Everyone is happy when the bridegroom is present. It is when the bridegroom is gone that people are sad. And the point of Jesus' answer was that He was the Bridegroom.

Jesus' answer is a warning about traditions and patterns upon which we become dependent. The new flow of His love in us cannot be satisfied in an old pattern of "religion" that ignores a hurting neighbor.

The flood of His presence enables each of us to break out of the accepted styles of ceremonies through radical life changes. We must make ourselves available.

Prayer

"Jesus, I am available for radical living. Help me see any changes I need to make in order to fulfill Your call to serve."

• MATTHEW 9:18-26 •

Matt. 11:28

"Come to me, all you who are weary and burdened, and I will give you rest."

A HANDLE FOR DISTRESS

Jairus was in terrible trouble; his daughter had just died. He pushed aside all acceptable manners and bolted uninvited into a party Jesus was attending.

"Behold, a ruler came and worshiped Him, saying, 'My daughter has just died, but come and lay Your hand on her and she will live'" (Matt. 9:18).

What a beautiful example of handling distress. First, Jairus worshiped. It was an inward awareness that caused him to stand in awe of Jesus; a confession that he had come to one greater than himself.

Second, Jairus came to the right source. He came to Jesus because he knew Jesus was adequate.

Third, Jairus believed and risked his reputation. His daughter had died, but he left the mourning party to search for Jesus. Because he believed.

Jairus sets a pattern for us to follow: seek the One who is adequate to meet our need.

Prayer

"Jesus, I come to You in my worst distress, because I believe You alone are enough to meet my need."

• MATTHEW 9:18-26 •

John 11:25
"I am the resurrection and the life. He who believes in me will live, even though he dies; and whoever lives and believes in me will never die."

THE REDEMPTION OF LIFE

Jairus, heavy with sorrow over the death of his daughter, came to Jesus. He came because he believed Christ could do for his daughter what no one else could do.

When Jesus arrived at Jairus' home, the mourning crowd was going through their rituals, and Jesus interrupted the procedures of death. "Make room," He said, "for the girl is not dead, but sleeping" (Matt. 9:24). The crowd laughed mockingly, but Jesus went in and raised her from the dead.

This girl, who actually experienced the Source of life within her, is an example of what Christ wants to do for us. Too often, we talk about the life of Christ but fall short of experiencing it. The facts are well known and a permanent part of our knowledge, but He is not experienced.

Christianity should be the actual life of Jesus within us. He causes us to live as we cannot live alone. It is His redemption, the redemption of life.

Prayer

"Jesus, redeem my life for You by actively living through me all the words and rituals I have passively stored away in my mind. Revive them in my heart. Speak them through my lips."

• MATTHEW 9:18-26 •

Matt. 9:21-22

"'If only I could touch his cloak, I will be healed.' Jesus turned and saw her. 'Take heart, daughter,' he said, 'your faith has healed you.'"

THE SOURCE OF LIFE

The Book of Matthew shows us people and their relationships to the life of Christ. First there was Jairus and his daughter (9:18-25).

But there is also the story of the woman who touched the Source of life in faith (v. 21). She had come and interrupted Jesus as He was going to raise Jairus' daughter from the dead. She knew if she could touch His garment, she would be healed. It was faith in action.

In desperation, the woman had no other place to turn. She saw that Christ was her only hope.

Let us all come to Christ with the kind of desperation that causes us to act on our faith, touching the Source of life in faith.

Prayer

"Jesus, I come to You, because I know without You there is no hope or power. My faith is in You, the Source of life."

• MATTHEW 9:27-31 •

Eph. 1:18
"I pray . . . that the eyes of your heart may be enlightened."

BLIND, BUT WITH VISION

Jesus was walking down the street when He was confronted by two blind men crying out to Him (Matt. 9:27). As Matthew relates, they receive their sight from Christ.

Although physically blind, these men had the vision of mercy. When Jesus walked by them, they cried out, "Son of David, have mercy on us!" (v. 27). They knew mercy was borne in Christ. They also knew Jesus was the prime expression of all the mercy of God extended to man.

These blind men had the vision of faith. In the course of conversation with them, Jesus said, "According to your faith let it be to you" (v. 29). Their faith was tested because Jesus was saying, "What happens to you will be determined by your faith."

These blind men also had the vision of evangelism. After they were healed, they brought another man in need to Jesus (v. 32).

We must ask ourselves if we have the visions of mercy, faith, and evangelism. Is there something in your life, like the healed blind men, that can only be explained by Jesus?

Prayer

"Jesus, open the eyes of my heart. Grant my request for clear visions of mercy, faith, and evangelism so that I, too, can experience the healing power of Your grace in my life."

• MATTHEW 9:32-34 •

Matt. 9:32-33

"A man who was demon-possessed and could not talk was brought to Jesus. And when the demon was driven out, the man who had been mute spoke. The crowd was amazed and said, 'Nothing like this has ever been seen in Israel.'"

UNABLE TO SPEAK

Jesus was constantly sought by the needy. Often, it was those who had experienced His healing that motivated others to seek Him. Two blind men had been healed, and they brought a man "mute and demon-possessed" to Jesus (Matt. 9:32-34). We are not told by what psychological means the devil had gripped him, but we know that it rendered him speechless.

I am sure there are times when we could identify with this man. We all have the facilities of expression but often find that the devil has gripped us by some psychological means, rendering us helpless in taking our stand for Christ.

Keeping the news of Christ to yourself keeps others from seeking Him. Certainly Christ, who delivered the mute man, can deliver us!

Prayer

"Jesus, I praise You for the gift of words. Enable me to speak as a means of expressing the good news of the gospel so that someone else will be motivated to find life in You."

• MATTHEW 9:32-34 •

Ps. 19:14

"May the words of my mouth and the meditation of my heart be pleasing in your sight, O Lord, my Rock and my Redeemer."

TONGUE IN CHECK

Matthew contrasts a man who could not speak at all and a group who spoke the wrong thing.

The mute man was brought to Jesus because Satan had a psychological grip on him that rendered him speechless. The Pharisees explained the miracle that Jesus performed by saying, "He casts out demons by the ruler of the demons" (Matt. 9:34).

The Pharisees' problem was keeping their words in check. James says, "If anyone among you thinks he is religious, and does not bridle his tongue but deceives his own heart, this one's religion is useless" (1:26).

A word spoken in the wrong place, in the wrong way, may void your Christian witness.

Prayer

"Jesus, I pray that You will save my tongue, as You have saved my heart, so that others may be saved for Your kingdom."

• MATTHEW 9:35-38 •

Ps. 139:13

"For you created my inmost being; you knit me together in my mother's womb."

MADE FOR HIM

Jesus said, "Therefore pray the Lord of the harvest to send out laborers into His harvest" (Matt. 9:38). This tells us something about ourselves.

We have been made by Him. If we check our life carefully, we discover His fingerprints all over us. He has handled us. We have been made to work His way. We fit into what He is all about.

God made each one of us. It is in relationship with Him that we discover who we are. If the relationship has been lost, we can recover what we do not have. We were made for Him, and He wants us.

Prayer

"Jesus, as a child created by You and for You, I give myself to wholehearted relationship with You, so that I may know me by knowing You."

• MATTHEW 9:35-38 •

Rom. 12:1
"Therefore, I urge you, brothers, in view of God's mercy, to offer your bodies as living sacrifices, holy and pleasing to God."

FULFILLING THE CALL

We often think of ministry as the accomplishment of a great feat, or the display of an amazing talent. In Matt. 9:35 it is related, "And Jesus went about all the cities and villages, teaching in their synagogues, preaching the gospel of the kingdom, and healing every sickness and every disease among the people."

The ministry Jesus performed was teaching, preaching, and miracles. The first line of the verse tells us that He went *everywhere*, flowing the life of God to His world. The Man called Jesus was filled with the Spirit of God, radiated the power of God, and ministered the presence of God to His world.

The truth is that God has called us to do exactly the same thing. We are not star performers, but we are to be persons filled with God, making a difference in our world. We must ask ourselves this question: "Am I fulfilling my call to minister like Jesus?"

Prayer

"Jesus, I pray for clear vision to look at my life and see if I am, in fact, living in fulfillment of Your personal call to me, as a minister for You."

• MATTHEW 9:35-38 •

Col. 3:12, 14

"Therefore, as God's chosen people . . . clothe yourselves with compassion, kindness, humility, gentleness and patience. . . . And over all these virtues put on love, which binds them all together in perfect unity."

FROM THE OVERFLOW

As Jesus reached out to people, He did not line His pockets, gather political support, or build an institution; He was motivated by love.

"But when He saw the multitudes, He was moved with compassion for them, because they were weary and scattered, like sheep having no shepherd" (Matt. 9:36).

The word "compassion" is the strongest word the Greek language has for pity. It describes people who are "deeply affected in their inward bowels." At the heart of their being, they have been moved.

Our relationships with others spring from many motives. Obligation, peer pressure, political power, and guilt are only a few. But Jesus called His disciples to minister from the overflow of love in the heart. When it happens for us, it will cost us a cross.

Prayer

"Jesus, only You can make my motives pure as You fill me with Your love. I am available to be filled to overflowing."

• MATTHEW 9:35-38 •

Luke 9:23

"If anyone would come after me, he must deny himself and take up his cross daily and follow me."

THE FELLOWSHIP OF HIS SUFFERING

Jesus had seen the condition of the multitudes, and it broke His heart.

Matthew tells us of the means that Jesus used for His ministry. In 9:38 he writes, "Therefore pray the Lord of the harvest to send out laborers into His harvest." He begins with prayer. Not just 15 minutes in the morning, but the kind of prayer that Jesus experienced as related within the words, "He was moved with compassion." It is deep from within and causes us to ache before the Father.

There are few who are willing to involve themselves in the life of Christ by taking on His compassion and burden. We want the "power of His resurrection," but are we willing to volunteer for the "fellowship of His sufferings" (Phil. 3:10)?

Prayer

"Jesus, I pray for more of a disturbance within so that my drive and motivation become an aching, compassionate heart, and I become a part of the fellowship of Your sufferings. I pray this for the Kingdom's sake."

• MATTHEW 10:1-4 •

1 John 4:14-15

"And we have seen and testify that the Father has sent his Son to be the Savior of the world. If anyone acknowledges that Jesus is the Son of God, God lives in him and he in God."

JESUS, THE ANSWER

Matt. 10:1-2 tells us of a sovereign God who has all authority. But this Father-God has delegated power to His Son Jesus for the purpose of redemption. Most of us have little trouble believing this truth because it all sounds theologically correct; God delegating power to His Son Jesus.

But there is startling news in the continued progression of power passed down. Verse 1 says, "And when He had called His twelve disciples to Him, He gave *them* power." And God, the supreme Authority, delegated authority to Christ so that *we* could receive authority for our lives. From a proper relationship with Christ the power of God is received for the believer's use. What a startling factor!

The problem comes when we do not utilize our greatest opportunity by responding in love to the One who is loving us. In Him is found the answer: divine power, which can meet the need of the heart's deepest cry. No wonder we keep repeating, "Jesus is the Answer."

Prayer

"Jesus, I know You are the Answer, even, and especially, for my specific needs. Help me rely more and more on the power of Your authority passed down to me, as the answer for all of my questions."

• MATTHEW 10:1-4 •

John 4:34

"My food . . . is to do the will of him who sent me."

BEFORE AND AFTER

Titles can be very superficial. But at times they can tell a significant story. There are two parallel statements in Matthew 10 that share such a story. In verse 1 it states, "And when He had called His twelve *disciples* to Him." Then in verse 2 it says, "Now the names of the twelve *apostles* are these" (italics added).

The significance is in what has taken place between these two statements. Jesus has taken the power within himself and transferred it to His disciples, renaming them apostles. There is a distinct definition for the word "apostle" that was well-known in Jesus' day. "The one who is sent is the same as the one who sent him." There were few apostles because it was such a powerful position. The apostle could act, make decisions, and determine the same as the one who sent him.

Jesus has called each of us to be an apostle. He wants to fill us with His Spirit so that we can be as He is. His power and life living within us can then flow through us to represent His person to our world. Let us stop and ask ourselves, "Is Jesus being seen in me?"

Prayer

"Jesus, I want You to be seen in me, as an apostle to my world."

• MATTHEW 10:5-15 •

Col. 2:6-7

"So then, just as you received Christ Jesus as Lord, continue to live in him, rooted and built up in him, strengthened in the faith as you were taught, and overflowing."

FREELY RECEIVE, FREELY GIVE

Each of our names could be written in Matthew 10. Jesus has looked for laborers to send into the harvest, and now He calls us by name. He takes His power and extends it to us so that we can duplicate His ministry. We now have the power to live His love and life-style.

But before Jesus sends His disciples into ministry, He gives detailed instructions on how the ministry should be accomplished. His first instruction is found in verse 8, "Heal the sick, cleanse the lepers, raise the dead, cast out demons. Freely you have received, freely give."

Jesus informs us that we are to take all that has been given to us and pour it into ministry to others. We are not to selfishly manipulate the power of God for our own carnal desires, but to use it for the sake of others. Jesus was our Pattern for such ministry. He never used the power of God for His own sake but made himself available to be expended for His world.

God has called us to the same selfless living.

Prayer

"Jesus, You have called me by Your grace and filled me with Your love. Keep me from clinging to the filling process so that what I receive not only flows in but spills out in overflow."

• MATTHEW 10:32-33 •

John 13:34-35
"Love one another. As I have loved you, so you must love one another. By this all men will know that you are my disciples, if you love one another."

BOLD LOVE

Jesus was more than a storyteller. He gave direct truth about distinct situations. Matthew 10 tells us the instructions Jesus gave in regard to daily living.

One of the great principles Jesus taught was to boldly stand for Him. In verse 32 He said, "Therefore whoever confesses Me before men, him I will also confess before My Father who is in heaven." He continues in the next verse with the negative aspects of this principle. "But whoever denies Me before men, him I will also deny before My Father who is in heaven."

The greatest tragedy for our world is to have churches full of good people who are not clear on their relationship with Jesus. One has to wonder if they really know Him personally or not.

Jesus teaches us that secret Christians do not exist. There is a boldness that comes from our relationship with Him that causes our world to know. This boldness, on purpose, communicates our fellowship with Him to our neighborhood. It is kind, loving, gentle, and caring, but bold. We should ask ourselves how long it has been since our faith made a difference in our neighborhood.

Prayer
"Jesus, give me boldness in my daily living so that my actions give clear evidence of Your presence in my life."

• MATTHEW 10:34-39 •

Eph. 4:1

"I urge you to live a life worthy of the calling you have received."

A CALL TO RADICAL LIVING

For some, Jesus was hard to tolerate. For many today, He still is. His call is so radical. In His instructions to His disciples concerning ministry, He said, "Do not think that I came to bring peace on earth. I did not come to bring peace but a sword" (Matt. 10:34).

As much as mankind might want, Christianity never fits into an easy chair. The symbol of Christianity still remains a cross. It is a call to disruptions, sacrifice, and radical living. One wonders how to fit the Christ who had no place to lay His head into the profit-making, selfish, 20th-century Christian.

It is not the *things* that make us bad, it is the inability to turn them loose for His sake. It is the priority structure inside each one of us that desires our comfortable wills more than His radical call. But the call is still there, awaiting our response.

Prayer

"Jesus, keep me away from desiring comfortableness so that I am not kept away from answering Your radical call to live near the Cross."

• MATTHEW 10:34-39 •

John 12:25
"The man who loves his life will lose it, while the man who hates his life in this world will keep it for eternal life."

LOSING TO FIND

There is always someone making selfishly motivated demands on me. I always feel so used.

Is Christ any different? He certainly makes demands on us, but they are out of concern for us. "And he who does not take his cross and follow after Me is not worthy of Me. He who finds his life will lose it, and he who loses his life for My sake will find it" (Matt. 10:38-39).

There are some startling differences in the demands that Christ makes. First, we know it is not for an hour or two, some money, or a little involvement. His demand is total. He wants all of our time, all of our money, and our total commitment to involvement. "He who loses his life for My sake."

Second, Christ's demand is not motivated out of selfish desires. He calls us to lose our life to Him; it is the only way we can possibly find it. He is also concerned because He knows the opposite is true: "He who finds his life will lose it." Losing in order to find—it is a paradox worth pursuing.

Prayer
"Jesus, I lose my life for the sake of finding it in You."

• MATTHEW 10:40-42 •

Matt. 25:40

"The King will reply, 'I tell you the truth, whatever you did for one of the least of these brothers of mine, you did for me.'"

LIKE JESUS

Success is such a hard item to measure in Christianity. The businessman knows when he is successful in business. The student knows of his success when the test is passed. The actor knows his success when he hears the applause.

However, success in Christianity is measured on a different standard. Jesus said, "And whoever gives one of the these little ones only a cup of water in the name of a disciple, assuredly, I say to you, he shall by no means lose his reward" (Matt. 10:42).

There are several elements to note carefully. One element is the symbol of a cup of water representing the ordinary that is highlighted in Christianity. Success is found in the normal, everyday living of normal, everyday people. Also, it is to "these little ones" that the cup is to be given because they cannot give it back.

An ordinary life poured out daily, without expecting anything in return, is success. Reward comes, but it is a total surprise because the deed is done without expectation—except that we become more like Him.

Prayer

"Jesus, I want my life to be poured out daily. Show me today the 'little one' in need of a cup of water so that I can offer it in Your name.'"

• MATTHEW 11:1-6 •

1 Cor. 10:13
"God is faithful; he will not let you be tempted beyond what you can bear. But when you are tempted, he will also provide a way out so that you can stand up under it."

JUST ENOUGH

John Wesley noted that there would be only two things that would destroy the movement of Christian holiness. First, we would expect too much; second, we would expect too little. Either failing would leave us empty in our souls.

Jesus takes the power within himself, gives it to His disciples, and sends them out to minister in that power. Matthew tells us how Jesus is going to spend His time. "Now it came to pass, when Jesus finished commanding His twelve disciples, that He departed from there to teach and to preach in their cities" (11:1). The word "their" agrees in number and in gender with the word "disciples." Jesus was going to spend His time ministering in the hometowns of the disciples.

Here is an example of Jesus not expecting too much. He knows that no prophet is without honor except in his own hometown (13:57). And Jesus cared enough about the details of the disciples' lives to take care of preaching for them.

It is the same in regard to our lives. Jesus is involved in every detail of daily living. He does not expect too much.

Prayer

"Jesus, I can serve today with the assurance that what You ask I can do, and what I do not have, You will provide."

• MATTHEW 11:1-6 •

John 14:27

"Peace I leave with you; my peace I give you. I do not give to you as the world gives. Do not let your hearts be troubled and do not be afraid."

EVEN IN THE DARK

For 400 years there had been no voice of God to Israel. From the end of the Old Testament (the Book of Malachi) to the beginning of the New Testament (the ministry of John the Baptist) the prophets of God had been silent.

Suddenly one of these strange prophets appeared on the banks of the Jordan River. He was a fearless individual, preaching a strong message with great boldness. He lived a strange life in the freedom of the wilderness, on a diet of locusts and wild honey. Due to his strong preaching, which upset the king, John the Baptist was placed in prison. It was a dungeon cell down by the Dead Sea in an abandoned fortress, probably underground and very small.

Matt. 11:2-3 says, "And when John had heard in prison about the works of Christ, he sent two of his disciples and said to Him, 'Are You the Coming One, or do we look for another?'"

When John was preaching on the banks of the Jordan River, he was absolutely sure who Jesus was; but now, in prison, things did not look the same because of depression and doubt. His emotions played tricks on him, causing questioning.

It is not wrong to question God in moments of depression and anxiety. Jesus didn't rebuke John. He has understanding, instruction, and praise for John. He is the same toward us. In the dark hours of dismay, Jesus cares and understands.

Prayer

"Jesus, I am grateful that You understand questions in the night, and that the light of Your love continues to shine even when I cannot see it."

• MATTHEW 11:1-6 •

Heb. 12:2-3

"Let us fix our eyes on Jesus, the author and perfecter of our faith, who for the joy set before him endured the cross, scorning its shame, and sat down at the right hand of the throne of God. Consider him who endured such opposition from sinful men, so that you will not grow weary and lose heart."

HE CARES

John the Baptist is someone with whom we can all identify. Persecution and imprisonment caused depression and anxiety to grip him. And what had seemed so sure to him at one time was suddenly doubtful.

Matt. 11:3 says that John "said to Him [Christ], 'Are You the Coming One, or do we look for another?'"

When trouble struck his life, John began to have questions in three areas. First, he began to question his experience. He had experienced Christ's presence when he baptized Him in the Jordan River. God the Father had spoken. But what was so real then seemed clouded in the fog of despair.

Second, he questioned his circumstances. John asked that inevitable question, "Why?" "Why did this happen to me?"

Third, he questioned his message. What John had preached in his sermons didn't seem to be happening in the present moment. He wondered if he had the right message.

We all have been faced with this kind of questioning. But John knew what to do. He went straight to Christ. He knew that the fears, doubts, and questions raised during depression could only be answered by Him. We too can seek Him in the middle of depression—because He cares!

Prayer

  "Jesus, my eyes are fixed on You, because with all the questions that surround me, I know You alone have the answers, and I am convinced that You care."

• MATTHEW 11:1-6 •

Prov. 3:5-6

"Trust in the Lord with all your heart and lean not on your own understanding; in all your ways acknowledge him, and he will make your paths straight."

THE ANSWER OF MIRACLES

Jesus will answer in times of questioning. When despair and doubts plague us in life, it is not a time for snap decisions. Seek the One who has the answers.

When John the Baptist was placed in prison, depressed and questioning, he sent two of the disciples to question Jesus. Matt. 11:4-5 says, "Jesus answered and said to them, 'Go and tell John the things which you hear and see: the blind receive their sight and the lame walk; the lepers are cleansed and the deaf hear; the dead are raised up and the poor have the gospel preached to them."

A part of the answer that Jesus gives to John in his depression is the answer of miracles. Notice the verb of each clause is present tense with continual action.

Jesus says that the answer to our question is the divine activity. What God has done in the past, He is doing again right now, and He will continue to do in the future. When in the pressure of depression, one may not feel the divine activity. But the reality of the divine support is as real when not felt as it is when felt. When our emotions are playing tricks on us, we can lean on the Christ who has acted, is acting, and will continue to act on our behalf.

Prayer

"Jesus, I lean on Your answer of miracles when my life is full of questions."

• MATTHEW 11:1-6 •

Ps. 25:10

"All the ways of the Lord are loving and faithful for those who keep the demands of his covenant."

DETERMINED BY FAITH

Decisions should never be based on the worst moments, but always on the best. This is what Jesus has said to John the Baptist, who is depressed in a prison cell.

Jesus says to John, "And blessed is he who is not offended because of Me" (Matt. 11:6). A literal translation would be, "Happy is the one who is not offended because of his relationship with Me."

John the Baptist had a working relationship with the redemptive process of God that flowed through the person of Christ. Although it was because of this relationship that he ended up in a prison cell, this should not have been a point of discouragement but an experience of praise for the God who was working out His will in the life of John.

If we could view our trials as an element of God's work in our lives, it would make a vital difference in our attitude. Perhaps we need to reevaluate our working relationship with Christ so that we are not offended by our situation but are pleased because of its part in shaping God's will in us.

Prayer

"Jesus, make known to me anything that may be coming between my relationship with You, so that I can look at life's ups and downs and be grateful for the part each plays in my becoming more like You."

• MATTHEW 11:7-12 •

Matt. 10:34

"Do not suppose that I have come to bring peace to the earth. I did not come to bring peace, but a sword."

VIOLENCE OF THE CROSS

In *Pilgrim's Progress*, John Bunyan tells of Christian who comes to the "little gate." Over the gate hangs a sign, which says, "Behold, I set before you an open door." Christian proceeded to knock on the door, but there was no answer. He began to beat and call out; still there was no answer. Finally, Christian yelled and hammered, and someone soon appeared.

When the keeper of the gate found out that Christian was going to the Celestial City, he quickly opened the gate, roughly grabbed Christian, and violently pulled him inside. He explained that just over the way there was a great tower where Beelzebub and his men dwelt. When someone tried to enter the gate, they threw darts in order to hinder him.

This is a picture of what Jesus is saying in Matt. 11:12, "And from the days of John the Baptist until now the kingdom of heaven suffers violence, and the violent take it by force."

There is no question that the entrance into the kingdom of God is violent. The very concept of the new birth is a violent consideration. We are to be pulled from one life pattern to another, roughly yanked from one life source to another, and planted deeply into one relationship out of another. All of this has to do with the violence of a cross. Christ is still violently saving people, to redeem from the violence of sin.

Prayer

"Jesus, I am willing to take up the violent rebirth of the Cross so that others can move away from the violence of sin and death."

• MATTHEW 11:20-24 •

Rom. 14:10, 12
"Why do you judge your brother? Or why do you look down on your brother? For we will all stand before God's judgment seat. . . . each of us will give an account of himself to God."

CALLED TO BE ACCOUNTABLE

Jesus uses a pattern in His upbraiding of the three cities in Matt. 11:20-24. He told them of their great opportunity and called them to responsibility. However, there is another factor: accountability.

The bottom line of justice is accountability; it is the only way to have order. Without it there is no growth or maturity. Where there is no accountability, there is spoilage.

We readily call our brother into accountability. Did he do the right thing? Did he make the most of his opportunities? Has he walked in the light he has received? Our concern should not be our brother, but ourselves. We are called into accountability by God. We face it now, and we will face it then, when we face Him.

Prayer
"Jesus, I want to live this day accountable to You, spending each moment wisely, as a responsible child and servant."

• MATTHEW 11:20-24 •

Matt. 10:8

"Freely you have received, freely give."

THE POSITION OF LIGHT

Jesus cries, "Woe to you, Chorazin! Woe to you, Bethsaida! For if the mighty works which were done in you had been done in Tyre and Sidon, they would have repented long ago in sackcloth and ashes" (Matt. 11:21).

Because these cities were given opportunity, the people are held responsible. Because they are responsible, they are held accountable.

First, there is accountability for the light of Christ, which had been displayed in these cities. God, being just, did not condemn them for their ignorance, only for what they knew. It isn't what we haven't learned that should concern us. We must tremble over what we know and have not followed.

Second, there is the factor of accountability of position. Jesus contrasts two Jewish cities with two Gentile cities. The Jewish cities received the high privilege of being selected by God for the position of being a channel of redemption.

We, too, have been honored in being selected by God for the high position of being used by Him. We have also witnessed the light of Jesus. Our response to *light* and *position* is to follow as He leads.

Prayer

"Jesus, let me focus clearly today on the light I have received and the position to which I have been called so that I can see if I am following where I have been led."

• MATTHEW 11:25-30 •

Matt. 11:25

"I praise you, Father, Lord of heaven and earth."

FOCUS ON GOD

Life isn't fair. We can do our best, and still things don't work out as planned.

Jesus is our Example of how to handle life's discouragements. In Matthew 11, there are three major blows to the ministry of Christ: John the Baptist questioned His Messiahship, the leaders of Israel rejected Him, and three major cities were indifferent to Him. What discouragement! Jesus' ministry collapsed around Him.

Look at the way Jesus handles this apparent defeat. Matt. 11:25 states, "At the time Jesus answered and said, 'I thank You, Father, Lord of heaven and earth.'" We notice that His first response is a prayer. By going to the One who cares, we tap into a resource that is waiting for us.

We also notice that the prayer is one of praise. The praise is not about His circumstances but about the Father whom He trusts. Learning to praise God for who He is will open our eyes to expanded resources.

Prayer and praise; it keeps our eyes off ourselves and on God.

Prayer

"Jesus, I purposefully take my eyes off my personal discouragements in an attitude of praise for who You are. When I look closely, I see Your power is much greater than my problems."

• MATTHEW 11:25-30 •

Isa. 40:10-11
"The Sovereign Lord comes with power, and his arm rules for him. . . . He tends his flock like a shepherd: He gathers the lambs in his arms and carries them close to his heart."

A TRUSTED SOVEREIGN FATHER

"Nothing is going right in my life! How do you expect me to be thankful?"

Matt. 11:25 says, "At that time Jesus answered and said, 'I thank You, Father, Lord of heaven and earth.'" Here is a picture of Christ, praising in the middle of His apparent failure in ministry. But the content of His thanksgiving is the key.

Jesus is thankful to the Father. His concentration was not on His problems but on His Father. We must not be sidetracked by our needs and lose sight of the One who has come to be our Father.

Jesus concentrates on the *sovereignty* of the Father. He is "Lord of heaven and earth." No problem is overwhelming when God, who is sovereign, is in control.

Prayer

"Jesus, I ask that You draw my attention to You today when I get stuck on the things that cause me to be anxious. I trust You with the unique complexities of my life, You who with the Father are Lord of heaven and earth."

• MATTHEW 11:25-30 •

Rom. 5:8

"But God demonstrates his own love for us in this: While we were still sinners, Christ died for us."

TRUST

A sovereign God may seem frightening if that God is going to interfere with our lives. How do we know what kind of wild demands He may make on us?

Jesus describes the sovereignty of God in the middle of a thanksgiving prayer. He prayed, "Even so, Father, for so it seemed good in Your sight" (Matt. 11:26). We see a picture of a sovereign God who is going to do exactly what pleases Him. And that is frightening only when we do not know the God of whom we are speaking.

We know that God is loving. In fact, we have discovered that He never acts except for our good. His first thought is always for us. He even sets aside what is good for himself in order that we may have what is good for us. We can trust a God like Him.

Prayer

"Jesus, I reaffirm my trust in You as I present myself to You for this day."

• MATTHEW 11:25-30 •

Eph. 2:18
"For through him we . . . have access to the Father."

THE CHARACTER OF GOD

Jesus said, "All things have been delivered to Me by My Father, and no one knows the Son except the Father. Nor does anyone know the Father except the Son, and he to whom the Son wills to reveal Him" (Matt. 11:27).

The privilege of revealing God to one is in Christ's hands. This is reason to be encouraged because we know the character of Jesus. He denies himself in favor of others. He loves children, helps the lame, and cares for the hungry. He turns down no one who comes to Him.

If Jesus is like this, then the revealing of God is open to us today. Jesus wants us to know God intimately.

Prayer

"Jesus, I pray You would reveal yourself to me through the ordinary experiences of my life."

• MATTHEW 11:25-30 •

2 Cor. 12:9

"My grace is sufficient for you, for my power is made perfect in weakness."

ATTITUDE SELECTION

The Bible teaches predestination and election. However, it is not that God chose one person to be saved and another to be damned. There is not a certain number of persons that God has selected.

The Bible teaches us that God has selected individuals based upon their attitudes. Matt. 11:25 says, "You have hidden these things from the wise and prudent and have revealed them to babes." Those who are depending on their own wisdom will not see the truth of God. Those who are willing to be dependent on Him will discover the reality of God as theirs.

Those who are open can be filled. Those who are isolated by their own logic, never see. It is the babe who depends on his mother that is fed, and the student who realizes his ignorance that is open to learning. It is a person who knows that his own power is not adequate for life that is willing to lean on the Christ who is available.

Prayer

"Jesus, my prayer is one of an awareness of my need to depend on You. Feed me from the Bread of Life, teach me with Your wisdom, and send me out to serve, not in my own strength but in the power of weakness made strong."

• MATTHEW 11:25-30 •

John 7:37

"If anyone is thirsty, let him come to me and drink."

WON BY ONE

Jesus' evangelism strategy was to win the leadership of Israel for the sake of winning Israel. If the leaders responded, then all of Israel would be ushered into the Kingdom. So He focused His attention on three of the major cities of Israel. If they were His, they would form an evangelistic base by which He could win Israel and a Gentile world.

However, in Matthew 11 we learn that the three cities and their leaders rejected Him.

Patiently, Jesus turned to a new strategy. It was an individual approach—one-on-one. Jesus stretched forth His hands and said, "Come to Me, all you who labor and are heavy laden, and I will give you rest" (v. 28).

Jesus' words, spoken to the individuals of Israel, are spoken directly to us today. He calls us one by one to himself.

Prayer

"Jesus, I have heard Your personalized, individual call to me. Help me today to find one to whom I can pass along Your call."

• MATTHEW 11:25-30 •

Ps. 62:5-6
"Find rest, O my soul, in God alone; my hope comes from him. He alone is my rock and my salvation."

COME—FOR REST

In Matthew 11 Jesus gives us three direct commands. They are not orders barked out by a top sergeant, but gentle whisperings of a loving Savior. He says, "Come to Me, all you who labor and are heavy laden, and I will give you rest. Take My yoke upon you . . . and you will find rest for your souls" (vv. 28-29).

He gives us an invitation: "Come to Me."

He extends to us His desire for participation in our life: "Take My yoke upon you." He wants intimate involvement in our life, but it is not a one-way street. We are to be involved with Him.

He guarantees that there is a location for us: "And you will find rest for your souls." There will be no frustration, no disappointment, and no dissatisfaction at the end of our search. We will find Him, for He is searching for us.

Prayer

"Jesus, thank You for the invitation to find rest in You and to participate in Your purpose in the world. I accept."

• MATTHEW 11:25-30 •

Rev. 19:9
"Blessed are those who are invited."

COME

If an invitation came sealed by the president of the United States, we would treat it differently than a warrant for our arrest. Any invitation is only as good as the one who is inviting.

Note this invitation: "Come to Me, all you who labor and are heavy laden, and I will give you rest" (Matt. 11:28). He will deal with each of us personally. He has said, "Come."

Notice, He has invited *"all* you." This invitation includes each one of us. It is an individual approach, a direct and personal extension of His hand.

He has invited all "who labor and are heavy laden." Those that life has burdened are invited. Those who have tried but have fallen short are invited. Perhaps, as we recognize ourselves, we can respond to the invitation to "come."

Prayer

"Jesus, I recognize myself as one who is invited to 'come.' I come, with the burdens of this day, for my rest in You."

• MATTHEW 11:25-30 •

Ps. 118:29
"Give thanks to the Lord, for he is good; his love endures forever."

IN EXCHANGE FOR LOVE

Isn't it great to be invited to participate in something special?

"Come to Me, all you who labor and are heavy laden, and I will give you rest. Take My yoke upon you and learn from Me" (Matt. 11:28-29). In these words, Jesus is extending an invitation to the one who is beaten, exhausted, and frustrated. He invites that one to come and participate.

He says, "Take My yoke." He wants us to exchange our heavy burden for His easy and light yoke of love. Love gives us freedom from the bondage of the law.

It is not a stagnant relationship. He is going to unfold himself to us. What an adventure!

Prayer

"Jesus, I come to You with all the responsibility weighing heavily on me and exchange it for Your yoke of love."

• MATTHEW 11:25-30 •

1 Pet. 4:13
"But rejoice that you participate in the sufferings of Christ, so that you may be overjoyed when his glory is revealed."

INVITATION TO PARTICIPATE

"Come to Me, all you who labor and are heavy laden, and I will give you rest. Take My yoke upon you and learn from Me," Jesus says in Matt. 11:28-29. He invites us to participate in His yoke.

Some think that the gospel is the removal of the yoke to the extent of kicking off the traces and having no obligations. But Jesus says He wants us to exchange the old yoke for His yoke.

The "old yoke" was the burden of legalism, which now is exchanged for a love relationship. No longer is it the fear of punishment when laws are broken; now it is the freedom of love, which goes beyond the law of duty. We are invited to share in His person, not the burden of religious ceremonies.

His invitation to participation is waiting.

Prayer

"Jesus, reveal Your personal love to me today so that those things that have become an act of duty can become a response to Your love instead."

• MATTHEW 11:25-30 •

Ps. 62:11-12
"One thing God has spoken, two things have I heard: that you, O God, are strong, and that you, O Lord, are loving."

THE UNFOLDING REVELATION

We all build walls to protect ourselves. But Jesus extends an invitation to us to participate in His yoke of fellowship with Him.

How open is He going to be with us? "Take My yoke upon you and learn from Me," He says (Matt. 11:29). He is not going to withhold any good thing from us. "Learn from Me" means He is going to be our personal Tutor as we begin an exciting investigation together.

What is the investigation? Just two verses earlier, Jesus told us that everything has been turned over to Him by His Father. He understands and knows the Father; He reveals the Father. Now He invites us to participate in the unfolding revelation of the person of God.

He wants to teach us all there is to know about God, when we are willing to learn.

Prayer

"Jesus, I am willing to learn. I want to participate in the unfolding revelation of the person of God."

• MATTHEW 11:25-30 •

Ps. 62:8

"Trust in him at all times, O people; pour out your hearts to him, for God is our refuge."

HE WILL GIVE IT

Jesus said, "Come to Me, all you who labor and are heavy laden, and I will give you rest. Take My yoke upon you and learn from Me, for I am gentle and lowly in heart, and you will find rest for your souls" (Matt. 11:28-29).

Jesus says, "I will give you rest," and "You will find rest." The reason we will locate it is because He will give it.

There will be no self-centered activity in this location. We will not be able to state what we have found, only what He has given. The lamb does not seek the shepherd.

God has leaped from His throne to get intimately involved in giving rest to us. The only opportunity that you and I have to find it is in Him, by setting aside pride in a willingness to receive from Him.

Prayer

"Jesus, I want to find the rest You offer for today and all the days that follow. I am open to finding it in the way You will personally give it to me."

• MATTHEW 11:25-30 •

Ps. 23:1-2

"The Lord is my shepherd, I shall not be in want. He makes me lie down in green pastures, he leads me beside quiet waters, he restores my soul."

REST TO ACTIVITY

Man seeks after God, only to be found by God. In the final analysis, there is no locating until there is surrender.

The location is "rest." Jesus said, "And you will find rest for your souls" (Matt. 11:29). Another translation of these phrases in Matthew says, "Come to me, and I will give rest to you, for I am restful, and ye shall find rest for yourselves" (*The Renaissance New Testament,* by Randolf Yeager).

The original Greek for the word "rest" is two words. Combined they mean "to rest up" or "to refresh oneself." An example is sleeping. This is a rest leading not to inactivity but to activity. The rest of which Jesus is speaking is a refreshment to the soul, bringing about the capacity for greater activity.

Christ does not take from us; He expands our capacity. We find ourselves enabled to live in greater ways as we find our rest in Him.

Prayer

"Jesus, I come for the rest You can provide to enable me for the task to which You have called me."

• MATTHEW 11:25-30 •

Ps. 25:4-5

"Show me your ways, O Lord, teach me your paths; guide me in your truth and teach me, for you are God my Savior, and my hope is in you all day long."

AN INVITATION TO ACCEPT

Jesus has extended an invitation to participate. He invites us to participate in location. This emphasis is found in Matt. 11:28-30. He says, "Come, take, and find." The climax comes in locating His rest. Verse 30 states, "For My yoke is easy and My burden is light."

The yoke of the Pharisee had been duty, ceremony, laws, and obligation. Contrasted against this was the easy yoke of Jesus, the revelation of the heart of God. He invites us to share in a love relationship with God.

Duty leaves us guilty, fearing that we have not done enough. Love gives us rest in knowing intimate relationship. Ceremony is empty, raising fears that it might not be real. Love gives us the person of Christ to embrace in companionship. Laws tell us what to do and judge us when we don't measure up. Love gives us power and guidance for right living.

Jesus offers His yoke with an invitation to accept.

Prayer

"Jesus, I want the rest that comes from an intimate relationship with You so that I may live in the power of Your love."

• MATTHEW 11:25-30 •

Ps. 13:5

"But I trust in your unfailing love; my heart rejoices in your salvation."

THE FREEDOM OF LOVE

The challenging call of Christ urges us to set aside our man-made religious traps and walk in the freedom of a relationship with Him. He calls it "My yoke." "For My yoke is easy and My burden is light" (Matt. 11:30).

Religious laws place restrictions on us, allowing us to go only so far. But love breaks the restraints and gives us freedom.

The law said you could hate but must not murder. Jesus said, "Live in love so that you don't want to murder." The law allowed lust but not adultery. Jesus instructed, "Live in love so that lust does not control your life."

He is calling us to an intimate love relationship with Him that will deliver us from internal sin, rather than restrain us with external obligations. His yoke is easy and His burden light.

Prayer

"Jesus, deliver me from internal sin. Place the freedom of Your yoke securely on me, and bind me to yourself."

• MATTHEW 12:1-8 •

John 8:7

"If any one of you is without sin, let him be the first to throw a stone at her."

AN ACCUSING SPIRIT?

The most difficult reality we face is to see ourselves as we really are. Personal honesty is hard to achieve.

Jesus is moving through the grainfields with His disciples, who are picking and eating grain. The crowds gather in anticipation of a conflict because it is the Sabbath, and the Pharisees leap to the attack. "Look, Your disciples are doing what is not lawful to do on the Sabbath!" (Matt. 12:2).

If we had lived in that time, with whom would we identify? What role would we have played? The Defender of truth and justice? One of the disciples? A follower? One who simply stands in the background and lets things happen? Might we have been a Pharisee?

Pharisaic qualities are hard to acknowledge in our own lives. An accusing spirit is so easy to justify when we have religious laws on our side. But remember, the Pharisees never extended redemption to the world.

Prayer

"Jesus, make known to me anything in my life that could be identified as an accusing spirit, and I will ask You to throw it out, for the sake of the Kingdom."

• MATTHEW 12:1-8 •

1 Tim. 1:15-16

"Christ Jesus came into the world to save sinners—of whom I am the worst. But for that very reason I was shown mercy so that in me, the worst of sinners, Christ Jesus might display his unlimited patience as an example for those who would believe on him and receive eternal life."

LIKE JESUS

The Pharisees were right for all the wrong reasons. They accused the disciples of breaking the Sabbath law, but Jesus was quick to defend His own.

Jesus says to the Pharisees, "But if you had known what this means, 'I desire mercy and not sacrifice,' you would not have condemned the guiltless" (Matt. 12:7). Jesus is emphasizing one of the Pharisaic qualities—"So righteous they were condemning." The problem was not in the law; rather it was in their motives.

For the Pharisee, the law was a whip to beat people rather than an ointment for healing. They viewed the law as a weapon of attack, rather than a means of rescue.

We must guard against becoming so "righteous" that everyone around us feels uncomfortable due to our unrighteous inner attitude.

Jesus was the only truly righteous man, yet publicans and sinners felt accepted by Him. Perhaps we would be more effective in influencing others if we were more like Jesus.

Prayer

"Jesus, make me a servant for the sake of others. Help me to be like You."

• MATTHEW 12:1-8 •

Rom. 3:23-24, 27

"All have sinned and fall short of the glory of God, and are justified freely by his grace through the redemption that came by Christ Jesus. . . . Where, then, is boasting? It is excluded. On what principle? On that of observing the law? No, but on that of faith."

NOT ENOUGH TO BE RIGHT

In dealing with the Pharisees, Jesus used the Old Testament. As they were ready to stone the disciples for picking and eating grain on the Sabbath Day, Jesus interrupted them by highlighting the fact that King David did the same thing in principle: "He entered the house of God and ate the showbread which was not lawful for him to eat" (Matt. 12:4). Jesus teaches that human value and need take precedence over ritual customs.

How can we be so right in our religious practices and so wrong in our daily attitudes? When we are so right that a relationship is broken and barriers are built, we are wrong.

It is not good enough to be right. We must be like Jesus, setting ourselves aside in order to pour life into our world.

Prayer

"Jesus, I have claimed my 'right to be right' many times. Today, help me to set aside my rightness for the sake of others."

• MATTHEW 12:1-8 •

Rom. 8:5-6

"Those who live according to the sinful nature have their minds set on what that nature desires; but those who live in accordance with the Spirit have their minds set on what the Spirit desires. . . . the mind controlled by the Spirit is life and peace."

IN THE DIRECTION OF GOD

For centuries the Pharisees looked for the Messiah. Jesus confronted them with the practices of God, but they could not see it. The Sabbath law was a main issue for them.

Jesus reminded them, "Or have you not read in the law that on the Sabbath the priests in the temple profane the Sabbath, and are blameless?" (Matt. 12:5). The work for the priests was double on the Sabbath because there were a variety of activities that were against the law. But worship of the person of God takes priority over the Sabbath laws.

It is easy for us to become so law-conscious that we are person-blinded. Many who pride themselves on keeping certain ethical standards do not have a relationship with the person of Christ. The law only points us in the direction of God. Our concentration should be on Him.

Prayer

"Jesus, draw my attention to You and away from the laws that served their purpose by drawing me to You."

• MATTHEW 12:1-8 •

1 Cor. 3:11

"For no one can lay any foundation other than the one already laid, which is Jesus Christ."

LORD OF THE CHURCH

An 18-year-old youth was in deep rebellion against authority. Drugs, stealing, and rebellion against his parents were all a part of his life. I confronted him one day and asked, "What is your problem?" His answer was that he did not want anyone telling him what to do—especially a preacher. When I asked his plans, he said he was going to join the marines. Can you imagine someone who does not want to live under any authority joining the marines?

Rebellion comes to all of us in many forms. Even the Pharisees had to face it.

Jesus stated, "For the Son of Man is Lord even of the Sabbath" (Matt. 12:8). He is the Author of the law.

It is easy to become so attached to practices at the church that we lose sight of the Lord of the church. Our concentration should be on Him.

Prayer

"Jesus, Lord of the Sabbath, I focus my attention on You. I am willing to go where You lead."

• MATTHEW 12:9-14 •

Prov. 31:20
"She opens her arms to the poor and extends her hands to the needy."

AN EXTENSION OF HANDS

Jesus is confronted by the Pharisees' piercing question, "Is it lawful to heal on the Sabbath?" (Matt. 12:10) as a man with a withered hand stands anxiously waiting.

Jesus tells of a sheep falling in a pit on the Sabbath and how it is permissible to rescue it. Pointing out that a man is of greater value than a sheep, He says, "Therefore it is lawful to do good on the Sabbath" (v. 12).

A principle is established by which we can measure our religious activities. We might call it "service worship over laws." The greatest act of worship to God is serving our fellowman.

By studying the life of Jesus, we discover that He conducted only one worship service as recorded in the Gospels. What did He do with His time? He fed the hungry, ministered to the sick, and helped the weak. The church should not be more concerned with how it rates in attendance competition than where it stands in ministry to human need. It is tragic when the church spends more energy on building programs than on a needy community.

God is calling us to be an extension of His loving hands. We may be tense, and there will certainly be those who are frowning; but the crowd is also waiting, wondering if His hands can reach them.

Prayer
"Jesus, take my hands and use them today as You did 2,000 years ago when You knelt to wash dirty feet."

• MATTHEW 12:1-14 •

Ps. 147:11
"The Lord delights in those who fear him, who put their hope in his unfailing love."

LIFE AT THE HEART

I once saw a building that was beautiful on the outside but being destroyed by termites on the inside. It reminded me of Matthew's picture of people who look religious on the outside but have no life at the heart.

There was a controversy between Jesus and the Pharisees over the Sabbath rules in Matt. 12:1-13. The Pharisees were deeply committed to keeping the laws of the Sabbath Day. (History tells us that thousands of Jews were killed in war because they would not defend themselves on the Sabbath.)

"Then the Pharisees went out and took counsel against Him, how they might destroy Him" (v. 14). It is a stunning contrast: obedience to Sabbath Day rules, but murder in their hearts.

An alcoholic in a community was tenderly confronted by the local pastor concerning his spiritual condition. His reply was, "Well, I am not all I ought to be, preacher, but I never eat meat on Friday!"

We must not justify ourselves by our outside activities. We must examine our spiritual heart condition, making sure our hearts are right with Him.

Prayer

"Jesus, closely examine my heart to see if I am living out of law or out of love."

• MATTHEW 12:1-14 •

Ps. 46:1
"God is our refuge and strength."

REST—LABOR

The first 14 verses of Matthew 12 center on an argument about the Sabbath Day law. But that is only a surface disagreement. The basic difference is in the doctrine of the kingdom of God. The Pharisees think that the kingdom of God is based upon labor—rest. Jesus knows that it is based upon rest—labor.

The Pharisees say that we must labor, struggle, try, work, do our duty, grit our teeth, and keep the law. If we perform sufficiently, then we will enter into the rest of the Kingdom. Jesus says that He came to reverse that process. First, He invites us to rest in Him, then we will be refreshed and ready to labor.

Many are exhausted from constantly trying to find acceptance with God. The message of the gospel has good news: come in surrender, bringing defeat and failure. Jesus will cleanse, fill, and enable for the work that needs to be accomplished.

Prayer

"Jesus, I surrender all my efforts to You and rest so that You can enable me to get up again and serve."

• MATTHEW 12:1-14 •

Ps. 91:1

"He who dwells in the shelter of the Most High will rest in the shadow of the Almighty."

REST, SO THAT . . .

The Pharisees did not grasp a fundamental truth of Christianity (Matthew 12).

In the Old Testament, the Sabbath Day, a day of rest, was the last day of the week. A person was to work all week, and then he deserved a day of rest. But in the New Testament, the day of rest is on Sunday, the first day of the week.

The gospel tells us that we must begin our week resting in Him. The work that we are to do throughout the week is not to earn a rest, but because of the rest. We rest in His resource so that we can labor.

The story of creation teaches this truth. God created for six days and then entered into the final day of rest. However, He created man on the close of the sixth day. Man's first day on earth was the day of rest. When man attempts to labor and then rest, he fails to recognize the new order that grace has brought.

We are not to live out of our own resources. Christianity is not what we do, it is Him. The resource of His person is available to live out through us.

Prayer

"Jesus, I rest in knowing it is not what I do for You, but what You do through me."

• MATTHEW 12:15-21 •

Ps. 139:14, 17
"I praise you because I am fearfully and wonderfully made. . . . How precious to me are your thoughts, O God!"

WORTHWHILE SELF-WORTH

Have you ever seen an overweight Barbie doll? Or one with a complexion problem? James Dobson tells us that the greatest crisis for every young person is in the area of self-esteem. Self-esteem seems to be based upon acceptance in three areas: looks, money, and intelligence.

If a person does not have good looks, but he does have money, he may still be able to be accepted. If one does not have good looks or money, but he does have intelligence, he can figure out how to get the first two.

In viewing the life of Christ as revealed by Matthew in 12:15-21, we see that He relates to us on the basis of the self-worth of Jesus; it has to do with His relationship with His Father. Jesus could withstand the rejection of the Pharisees because He was accepted by the Father. The fickleness of the crowds did not shake Him because the love of the Father was unshakable.

True self-worth can only be experienced when it is derived from a proper relationship with God.

Prayer

"Jesus, it is easy to evaluate myself by the measuring stick of the world in which I live. I pray for a clearer focus on Your thoughts of me, so that my feelings of value come from You alone."

MATTHEW 12:15-21

Matt. 12:18

"Here is my servant whom I have chosen, the one I love, in whom I delight."

DOING IT HIS WAY

A struggle for every young person is in the area of self-esteem. Many long-lasting problems are created because many young people do not have proper self-worth.

Often we have viewed the problem simply as too little self-esteem. But equally destructive is too much self-esteem. The Bible talks to us about a perverted self-image that views itself as God, using the word "carnal."

This carnal nature is a perverted self-sovereignty that wants to take the place of God. In an individual that thinks too much of himself, self-esteem runs wild.

In our own lives we have often been guilty of playing the role of God. We have allowed Him to maintain His sovereignty in the universal decisions, but in our own lives we have become sovereign. We have sung songs stating, "I did it my way."

Matthew has given us a picture of proper self-esteem; it is found in Jesus. He is in relationship with His Father as we are to be in relationship to Him. Jesus derived His self-worth from the Father. If we are willing to honestly look at the basis for our self-worth, we can truly find ourselves in Him.

Prayer

"Jesus, I find myself in You, the One who has chosen, loved, and delighted in me."

• MATTHEW 12:15-21 •

Matt. 3:17

"And a voice from heaven said, 'This is my Son, whom I love; with him I am well pleased.'"

CHOSEN BY HIM

Discovering who we are is directly related to discovering who God is, and our relationship to Him. The Bible teaches that we derive our worth from Him. Mankind has no worth except as he has been made in God's image and is thereby related to Him.

This was true for Jesus, the Man. Matthew reveals this from the Book of Isaiah: "Behold, My Servant whom I have chosen" (Matt. 12:18).

In the days of the Pharisees' rejection of His ministry, Jesus must have derived self-worth from the fact that He was a chosen servant of God. It is important to notice that He was *chosen*. This was not a random, accidental choosing, but a specific selection because Jesus was the only one who qualified for the position of Messiah. Since Isaiah relates this fact in the Old Testament, we know that He was chosen long before a cross; it was an eternal choice of God.

God has done the same for each of us. "He chose us in Him before the foundation of the world" (Eph. 1:4). We each are one of His special chosen servants; and we each are valuable to Him.

Prayer

"Jesus, for the days when I feel worthless, I will find hope in the fact that I have been chosen by You."

• MATTHEW 12:15-21 •

John 15:9

"As the Father has loved me, so have I loved you. Now remain in my love."

AGGRESSIVE LOVE

We are told that a human can tolerate just about any circumstance if he is convinced that he is loved. An individual's self-worth is so deeply connected to needing love that rejection can destroy one's self-esteem.

Matthew quoted Isaiah, who was writing concerning the Father's feelings for Jesus the Son. "Behold, My Servant whom I have chosen, My Beloved in whom My soul is well pleased" (Matt. 12:18).

Those words "My Beloved" are very significant. They literally mean, "You are the Object of My love." No wonder Jesus was able to go through such difficult times. He was deeply loved by the Father.

God feels the same way about us. The Bible teaches us that all the compassionate love Jesus experienced from the Father is also ours through Christ (John 15:9). He has proven it in action. Jesus has done nothing but work on our behalf, at His own expense.

We are intimately and aggressively loved. We are valuable to God! We can express our gratitude by loving Him in return.

Prayer

"Jesus, in gratitude for Your endless and unexplainable love for me, I offer my life in service, as an advertisement of Your aggressive and all-inclusive love."

• MATTHEW 12:15-21 •

Rom. 12:10, 13
"Be devoted to one another in brotherly love. Honor one another above yourselves. . . . Share with God's people who are in need."

AVAILABLE

God called Jesus to a mission that only the Son of God could accomplish. The method Jesus used to carry out His mission was servanthood, as related in Matt. 12:19-20: "He will not quarrel nor cry out, nor will anyone hear His voice in the streets. A bruised reed He will not break, and smoking flax He will not quench."

We note that the method involves "servanthood, not quarreling." Also, His method is that of "servanthood, not exploitation." The words "bruised reed" and "smoking flax" are symbolic of those people who were used or were downtrodden. The Pharisees used these people for their own schemes, manipulating them in order to line their own pockets.

However, Christ had a different method: servanthood. He did not come to use us but to serve us. His plan is to join with us as a partner in life. Jesus died because of His love. He wants to serve through us, but we have to be available.

Prayer
"Jesus, I am available. Love through me."

• MATTHEW 12:15-21 •

John 3:16
"For God so loved the world that he gave his one and only Son, that whoever believes in him shall not perish but have eternal life."

SERVICE TO ALL

It is interesting to watch a teenager who senses tremendous peer pressure to be like his intimate group of friends. There is a large society that is many times larger than the size of this group that pressures him to be different, but he only responds to the pressure of a few. It is amazing how narrow we often are in our approach to life.

Jesus set the pattern for us of "servanthood, not quarreling" and "servanthood, not exploitation." Now consider that it was "servanthood not to a few." Matthew quotes from the Old Testament with this statement: "And in His name Gentiles will trust" (Matt. 12:21).

Jesus came to win the world. The Jews, who wanted to claim exclusive rights to the gospel, had to give way to the sweeping need of all people. "For God so loved the world" (John 3:16).

We must never find ourselves ministering only to people like us—on our social level, wearing our style of clothing, and having our level of education. The gospel will not allow it. Jesus taught "servanthood not to a few" but to everyone.

Prayer

"Jesus, open my eyes to those outside my inner circle so that I may see them as You see them: the reason for offering yourself."

• MATTHEW 12:22-24 •

Ps. 121:1-2
"I lift up my eyes to the hills—where does my help come from? My help comes from the Lord, the Maker of heaven and earth."

BEYOND TODAY

The Bible tells us that history is in a linear process. Everything is moving to a meaningful end under the divine guidance of a sovereign God. Man was created by God, and while he has a free will to respond as he chooses, the ultimate plans of God for the world will be accomplished.

It may be that you do not see the significance of this truth in your own life. You may have become like the Pharisees in the Gospel of Matthew 12:22-24. They lived in their own political structure, thinking they were in control of the events of their history. They were so bogged down in temporal activities that they missed the eternal activities of a sovereign God. God is calling us to live beyond the mundane events of today.

Prayer
"Jesus, I purposefully lift my eyes to You, Creator of the universe of which I am a significant, and yet infinitely small, part. I want Your plans to be accomplished, in some way, through me."

• MATTHEW 12:22-24 •

Josh. 24:15
"Choose for yourselves this day whom you will serve . . . But as for me and my household, we will serve the Lord."

WHO DO I SERVE?

The Bible tells us that the events of our daily lives are part of a tremendous battle. King Jesus and the satanic forces are battling for the same territory: you and me.

The conflicts in which we are involved are rooted in the battle between the two kingdoms. Paul told us that "we do not wrestle against flesh and blood" (Eph. 6:12). This gives new perspective concerning the ordinary events in our daily living. The influence of our lives is greater than we realize. Our attitudes, our smile, or the helpful service are acts in the battle of the Kingdom.

A crisis decision is made at an altar to enter the kingdom of God. But the battle is fought on the stage of daily living. Who I serve is determined there.

We must ask ourselves daily, "Who do I serve?"

Prayer

"Jesus, in every decision I make today keep me aware of the choice I have made above all choices—to serve You."

• MATTHEW 12:22-24 •

Gal. 2:20
"I have been crucified with Christ and I no longer live, but Christ lives in me. The life I live in the body, I live by faith in the Son of God, who loved me and gave himself for me."

AND THE ANSWER IS . . .

The people of Jesus' day were confronted with a great question: "Could this be the Son of David?" (Matt. 12:23).

A demon-possessed man was brought to Jesus (v. 22). He was blind and mute, but Jesus delivered him. David was an Old Testament king over Israel, and it had been prophesied that there would come one from his lineage that would reign as King forever. Is Jesus Christ this King of the kingdom of God?

There are those who would answer that He is not. In fact, some said that He was in cooperation with Beelzebub, the ruler of the demons, saying that He was not casting out demons but catering to them.

If we allow our lives to be dominated by sin, have we not joined those who curse Him? As we participate in those things that are directly opposed to what He teaches, are we not taking a stand against Him? What will be the answer in response to His love?

Prayer

"Jesus, my answer is a daily reaffirmation of faith in You who have been sent to save me."

• MATTHEW 12:22-24 •

John 6:41
"I am the bread that came down from heaven."

"IS IT YOU?"

Jesus had healed a demon-possessed man, and the crowds responded. "And all the multitudes were amazed and said, 'Could this be the Son of David?'" (Matt. 12:23).

It was the question of the hour. Jesus was being examined in light of the Messiah's credentials.

The negative structure of the question ("This couldn't be the Messiah, could it?") anticipates a negative response. Jesus doesn't *really* fulfill the description of what the Messiah should be. He isn't even a great military leader, only a miracle worker. He doesn't associate with the right people.

Perhaps we have all been guilty of this view of Jesus: viewing Christ and His Church as good, but doubting because of continued human sufferings. As a sovereign God, Jesus doesn't act quite as we think He should. But, taking another look at Him, we see His cross and His obvious love for us. And the question, "Is it You?" is answered with a resounding, "Yes!"

Prayer

"Jesus, I place my faith in You, not only when things are going well, but also when things cause me to want to question, 'Is it You?'"

• MATTHEW 12:22-24 •

Ps. 47:7

"For God is the King of all the earth; sing to him a psalm of praise."

HE IS THE KING!

There are all kinds of opinions concerning the person of Christ. Those who were touched by the ministry of Jesus, as recorded in Matthew, had two opinions. Some said, "He is *not* the Son of David." Others, "Maybe He is the Son of David."

Jesus set the record straight when He stated, "But if I cast out demons by the Spirit of God, surely the kingdom of God has come upon you" (12:28).

The very fact that Satan's kingdom is invaded, the lives of men are being delivered, and the kingdom of God is growing tells us He is the King of the kingdom of God. He has come. The kingdom of God is not only for the future but a present reality. It is a growing, developing entity. The head of the Kingdom army has come. Jesus is King!

Prayer

"Jesus, I submit my life unto the authority of Your Kingship, for my participation in Your kingdom on earth and the celebration of Your kingdom in heaven."

• MATTHEW 12:22-24 •

John 3:17-18

"For God did not send his Son into the world to condemn the world, but to save the world through him. Whoever believes in him is not condemned, but whoever does not believe stands condemned already."

DECIDE TO DECIDE

In Jesus' day, as in ours, there were a variety of people who tried to be neutral about the kingdom of God. However, the decision not to decide, decides against.

Often we have resisted any kind of pressure that would force us to commit our lives to Christ. "No one is going to demand commitment from me!" we have yelled. We would not yield to that kind of request, believing that each person has a right to his own individuality!

However, it must be stated that commitment is inevitable. While no one can force us to decide one way or the other, we will eventually decide. A vivid picture of this is given throughout the Scripture, but especially in Matt. 12:22.

The Pharisees, who decided against Jesus, proved that deciding for the church and religious activities does not necessarily mean deciding for Jesus. On the other hand, the crowds were attempting to be neutral, which actually decided "against," since it was not a decision "for." The disciples, however, made their decision *for* Christ.

We must each decide where we fit in. Are we "for," "against," or "neutral"? We must decide to decide.

Prayer

"Jesus, my decision is for You, who came to live, die, and rise for my sake."

• MATTHEW 12:22-24 •

Ps. 40:8
"I desire to do your will, O my God."

WILLING FORGIVENESS

One of the most distressing verses found in the Bible is in Matt. 12:32: "Whoever speaks against the Holy Spirit, it will not be forgiven him, either in this age or in the age to come."

To even come close to understanding this statement, we must first understand the context. The Pharisees have totally rejected Jesus in their hearts, as recorded in Matthew 12. Nothing He could do now would please them. They have even plotted to murder Him (v. 14).

Jesus casts out a demon from a blind and mute man. The Pharisees, due to obstinate spiritual blindness, felt compelled to explain how Jesus does His miracles, by saying, "This fellow does not cast out demons except by Beelzebub" (v. 24). The Pharisees linked Jesus with the lowest filth. Their hearts were filled with rebellion.

As long as there is rebellion in the heart against the Holy Spirit, there can be no forgiveness. Reconciliation to God must be prompted by a heart of repentance. He is willing to forgive when we come with willing hearts.

Prayer

"Jesus, shine a bright light on anything in me that could reflect a rebellious spirit, and purge it by Your grace. I want to stand clean in the light of Your forgiveness."

• MATTHEW 12:25-31 •

John 7:38

"Whoever believes in me, as the Scripture has said, streams of living water will flow from within him."

ALL

Jesus told the Pharisees, "Therefore I say to you, every sin and blasphemy will be forgiven men, but the blasphemy against the Spirit will not be forgiven men" (Matt. 12:31).

These are shocking words to a person who longs to know God intimately. It is deeply disturbing to think that there might be a time when we are no longer forgivable. It is even more disturbing to realize who spoke the words.

If the Pharisees in their narrowness had screamed these words, we could understand it. But Jesus? We have seen Him in His great love, holding nothing back in order to redeem us. He set aside His glory in order to spill His blood to provide redemption. This is the kind of love that forgives at all cost, not at all the kind of love to hold back on forgiveness.

But the problem is not with Jesus; it is with you and me. Forgiveness is not withheld, it is unreceived. This is the sin that is against the Spirit and in the spirit of man: nonacceptance of Jesus' offer.

Prayer

"Jesus, for today and the tomorrows, I make myself available to receive, in gratitude and praise, all You have to offer."

MATTHEW 12:25-31

Ps. 51:1-2

"Have mercy on me, O God, according to your unfailing love; according to your great compassion blot out my transgressions. Wash away all my iniquity and cleanse me from my sin."

PERSONALLY YOURS

To think about the eternal, final consummation of life or the absolute, final end of the age is sobering. Jesus' words in Matt. 12:31 are far from comforting. He states, "Therefore I say to you, every sin and blasphemy will be forgiven men, but the blasphemy against the Spirit will not be forgiven men."

One of the factors that is so disquieting about this statement is to whom it is spoken. If Jesus had spoken exclusively to the Israelites, we could feel relieved. Certainly they deserved every bit of scorn Jesus could give, as their history was one of consistent rebellion and disobedience.

Maybe "Therefore I say to you" is directly related to the Pharisees. They certainly should receive all of the fierce judgment of Jesus. But it is that word "you" that is bothersome.

The words of Jesus are eternal in their impact. They leap from the pages of the Bible and come personally into our world, confronting us with their truth. And the word "you," in reference to Jesus' words of sin that cannot be forgiven, could be replaced with my name or yours.

Forgiveness is ours, but not in a resistant, rebellious, self-centered state, which is blasphemy to the Spirit. Jesus calls us by name to surrender anything that might be resistant or self-centered so that He can personally live in us.

Prayer

"Jesus, submerge me in the bath of Your forgiveness. Wash away any self-centeredness that still hangs on today. Clean me out so that there is only room left for You."

• MATTHEW 12:31-37 •

Ps. 51:10

"Create in me a pure heart, O God, and renew a steadfast spirit within me."

CREATION FROM WITHIN

There is confusion surrounding the concept of the unpardonable sin. But if we read carefully from verse 31 to verse 37 of Matthew 12, we see a flow of truth that forms a proposition. "The heart is the producer of all things in life; therefore, it must ultimately be heard and be held accountable."

In dealing with the unpardonable sin, Jesus is not speaking to the deed of sin. There are sins that a person commits, but there is also a condition of sin from within. The outward deed is a symptom of the inward condition.

The Pharisees, addressed in chapter 12, are good examples of those who have corrected the outward deeds of sin but have given no attention to the condition of their hearts.

To those of us who may be bordering on such neglect, Christ is extending His forgiveness and cleansing. He wants to create within a new heart.

Prayer

"Jesus, make known to me any outward deeds that would reflect an inward heart disease, and create in me a pure heart."

• MATTHEW 12:31-37 •

Matt. 12:35
"The good man brings good things out of the good stored up in him, and the evil man brings evil things out of the evil stored up in him."

GOOD TREE, GOOD FRUIT

Jesus teaches us in Matt. 12:31-37 that the heart is the producer of all things in life; therefore, it must ultimately be heard and be held accountable.

As He begins to describe this principle to us, He begins by stating in verse 33, "Either make a tree good and its fruit good, or else make the tree bad and its fruit bad; for a tree is known by its fruit."

Jesus states that good and bad cannot be combined. The condition of the fruit and the tree are one.

What we are in our inner heart is what we really are. Our inner heart will demonstrate itself in living. Ultimately, there is no way to stop it. "Be sure your sin will find you out" (Num. 32:23).

This is why Jesus' call to have a pure heart continues. He alone can give it to us. All we have to do is ask.

Prayer

"Jesus, store me up with the goodness of Your love so that my life's accomplishments are an outward manifestation of Your love within."

• MATTHEW 12:31-37 •

Phil. 2:12-13

"Therefore, my dear friends, as you have always obeyed . . . continue to work out your salvation with fear and trembling, for it is God who works in you to will and to act according to his good purpose."

INSIDE CONDITION

The unpardonable sin, found in Matt. 12:31-32, has been a fearful concept for many. Some of us have been taught that during the course of our life, we might commit one sin too many. No one knows the magic number. This, we believe, could be the sin that "breaks the camel's back." And God, so affected by "one sin too many," will turn His back on us forever.

However, careful study of the context of these verses can clear the air of all fear. God is not retreating from us; He is marching aggressively toward us. There is no deed of sin worse than others. They are all the same in His sight. He has sacrificed all to win us, and He is not about to let go now.

The unpardonable sin is not a deed we have done; it is what we have become. It does not deal with an outside action; rather, it deals with an inside condition: the condition of the inner heart.

We cannot allow the devil to sidetrack us with minor issues. Holiness is not merely doing the right thing; it is being right from the inside out. The change of life we need is in our heart. Jesus deals with changing our inward lives as we make ourselves available to Him.

Prayer

"Jesus, continue to work in me so that You can work through me."

• MATTHEW 12:31-37 •

Heb. 12:10
"God disciplines us for our good, that we may share in his holiness."

INSIDE OUT

In the spiritual realm, a person does not die from the outside in; he dies from the inside out.

Jesus' ministry on earth was so penetrating because His emphasis was the heart. To get close to Jesus was to have the deep inner heart revealed.

How tragic to spend a lifetime developing the moral disciplines to be right in outward actions, but neglecting the poison spilling from a sinful heart. This is why social reform without the gospel's redemptive heart-change brings frustration. The social issues of abortion, drug addiction, alcoholism, and pornography have to do with the inner heart.

The good news is that Jesus Christ died to cleanse the inner fountain of man's life. Rather than merely treating the "skin rash" of outward actions, Jesus wants to deal with the cancer of the heart. Heart purity is the purpose for which He came.

Most of us find it difficult to deal with a radical change in our self-centered heart. It is so hard to surrender all that we are, but Jesus calls us from the inside out so that all He is can come in.

Prayer

"Jesus, at all costs, burn through the exterior and get to my heart. I ask for Your discipline so that I too may walk in holiness."

• MATTHEW 12:31-37 •

Acts 4:31

"After they prayed, the place where they were meeting was shaken. And they were all filled with the Holy Spirit and spoke the word of God boldly."

FILLED WITH HIMSELF

It was a bold, slap-in-the-face statement when Jesus told the Pharisees they had committed the unpardonable sin (Matt. 12:31-32).

The Pharisees were the most righteous men of their day. They built their houses close to the church so that they would never have to miss (even during a snowstorm). They tithed their money to the penny.

It is interesting to note that Jesus accused this pious group of committing the unpardonable sin. This sin was not what the Pharisees had done; rather it was what they had become. While outward actions were proper, they had died in their hearts.

The Bible calls this the carnal nature, and there is only one possible deliverance from it. Jesus must cleanse the heart and fill it up with himself. He is available to all who will ask.

Prayer

"Jesus, fill me with Your Holy Spirit so that my heart, which in itself is weak, will be alive in You."

• MATTHEW 12:31-37 •

Ps. 26:2
"Test me, O Lord, and try me, examine my heart and my mind."

HEART EXAM

Who has the capacity for committing the unpardonable sin? (Matt. 12:31-32).

Jesus is addressing the Pharisees in these verses. They had committed this sin, not because of what they had done, but because of what they had become.

Today we see it is not the pagan on the street or the prostitute in the lower end of town who has the capacity to sin in unpardonable measure. It is the religious person who comes to church faithfully; the one who is moral in his activities. He is surrounded by the Word of God, sitting in a worship atmosphere, applauding the growth of the church. However, he sits in his pew week after week and dies in his heart.

The call of Christ becomes commonplace to this faithful churchgoer. The values of the gospel are treated lightly. The heart builds its resistance, and deadness takes place. Self-centered interests take precedence over the importance of the will of God. The heart is in a gradual death process.

We must have the courage to examine our heart for anything less than total commitment.

Prayer

"Jesus, I am available for examination. Make me aware of anything in me that keeps me from full surrender."

• MATTHEW 12:31-37 •

Ps. 17:3

"Though you probe my heart and examine me at night, though you test me, you will find nothing; I have resolved that my mouth will not sin."

IN *YOUR* HEART

Jesus closes His teaching on the subject of the unpardonable sin with these words, "For by your words you will be justified, and by your words you will be condemned" (Matt. 12:37).

John Fletcher, who was Wesley's theologian, tells us there are four justifications. First, there is a justification at birth. Everyone is born in sin, and yet if the newborn baby dies, he goes to heaven. The baby is covered by the prevenient grace of God.

Second, there is the justification of believing. Because I have voluntarily disobeyed God, I have nullified the justification at birth. I must come now in repentance and be forgiven for my sins.

Third, there is the justification of bringing forth fruit. James says, "Faith without works is dead" (2:20, 26, cf. 17). I am not saved by works, but they do give evidence that I have been saved.

The fourth is called final justification. It is what Jesus is talking about in verse 37. The words that come from our mouths are evidence of what is in our hearts. Thus, it will be the condition of our hearts that will determine the final justification.

What are you like in your heart?

Prayer

"Jesus, I praise You with all I have for Your grace, which can purify my heart and keep me pure."

• MATTHEW 12:31-37 •

John 15:4

"Remain in me, and I will remain in you. No branch can bear fruit by itself; it must remain in the vine."

DOWN INSIDE

The conclusion of the teaching on the unpardonable sin has to do with what the heart reveals about our attitudes (Matt. 12:37).

Attitudes are not produced by circumstances. Attitudes come from the heart. Circumstances set a stage for drawing out what we are really like on the inside. Then, when we are embarrassed, we blame others. But it all comes from our own hearts.

A hateful attitude replies, "If they had done to you what they did to me, you would hate them too!" But hatred is not produced by circumstances; it comes from the heart.

What a shame to spend a lifetime blaming others; moving from one section of town to another, quitting one job to take another. The problem always goes with us. It is the condition of our heart.

We must carefully examine our hearts. Our response to any situation can only reach as high as what's down inside.

Prayer

"Jesus, give me grace to remain in You, attached to the Source of life, so that my attitude is not altered by my circumstances."

• MATTHEW 12:31-37 •

1 Thess. 4:3

"It is God's will that you should be sanctified."

WHAT'S REALLY IN THE BASEMENT?

C. S. Lewis relates the procedure of finding out what is in the basement. It would seem to be an easy process; simply going down the basement stairs and looking around. But there are careful instructions.

To *really* find out what's in the basement, the door must be left ajar. After returning to bed, get up at three o'clock in the morning, tiptoe down the basement stairs, and quietly flip on the light. It is in these unguarded moments that the true inhabitants—rats—appear in some basements.

In apologizing for some action, some of us say, "I am not really like that. It was an 'unguarded moment.'" Could it be that the way we are in the unguarded moment is the way we really are? It is a difficult truth, but it is what Jesus has been telling us about our hearts (Matt. 12:37).

Jesus died to cleanse our hearts. When the heart is not right, responses to the situations of life are not right. It is time we bring the wrong deeds to Jesus for forgiveness, and our hearts to Him for cleansing.

Prayer

"Jesus, I want Your sanctifying grace, even in the basement of my heart, so that in my unguarded moments all that comes out is You."

• MATTHEW 12:31-37 •

Col. 3:1, 3

"Since, then, you have been raised with Christ, set your hearts on things above, where Christ is seated at the right hand of God. . . . For you died, and your life is now hidden with Christ in God."

WHAT SPILLS OUT?

A speaker in the chapel of Asbury College walked to the front of the pulpit, holding a plastic glass in his hand. He had filled the glass with water; everyone could see it. He had asked one of the faculty members to assist him by standing by his side, placing both of her hands on his arm, and shaking his arm. Naturally, water spilled out onto the chapel floor.

The speaker quickly asked his assistant to answer this question: "Why did water spill out of the glass?" At first she thought it was because she had shaken his arm. But as she thought it through, she realized it was because of the water contained in the glass. Water spills out of a glass because water is in it.

This is the truth Jesus is teaching in Matt. 12:37. Someone or something shakes us, and terrible things spill out—not because of the shaking, but because of what is contained within. Jesus, because of His death, is the only one who can change us from the inside out, so that when we are shaken, what spills out is Him.

Prayer

"Jesus, I praise You for grace that hides my life in Yours, so that what spills out on others can draw them to You."

• MATTHEW 12:38-42 •

Col. 3:16

"Let the word of Christ dwell in you richly as you teach and admonish one another with all wisdom, and as you sing psalms, hymns and spiritual songs with gratitude in your hearts to God."

HIM AND HIS WORD

Sadly, the Pharisees of yesterday were much like we are today. In Matt. 12:38 it says, "Then some of the scribes and Pharisees answered, saying, 'Teacher, we want to see a sign from You.'"

We cannot criticize the Pharisees for asking for a sign. After all, don't we demand verification for that to which we are giving our lives? Shouldn't we have some standard of truth if we are to believe?

There is nothing wrong with signs. The miracles Jesus performed were vivid signs, pointing to His Messiahship. The disciples, in the Book of Acts, were reported as doing "signs and wonders." It isn't that signs are wrong, but enough is enough!

How much more could the Pharisees demand from this Christ than what He had already accomplished. The record is there. He raised the dead, walked on the water, calmed the sea, healed the lepers, and cast out demons. What more could they possibly demand?

But sign-seekers are never satisfied. They always want to see one more sign.

Lest you or I become more concerned about what God can do for us rather than who He is in our lives, we must focus our attention away from the sign and on the Giver of the sign; looking not at what He does, but who He is.

Prayer

"Jesus, thank You for Your Word, which allows me to see You clearly, not only for what You do, but for who You are."

• MATTHEW 12:38-42 •

1 John 2:6
"Whoever claims to live in him must walk as Jesus did."

WHAT ABOUT JESUS?

Jesus had an answer for the sign-seekers. Matthew records the answer in 12:39: "But He answered and said to them, 'An evil and adulterous generation seeks after a sign, and no sign will be given to it except the sign of the prophet Jonah.'"

When we study this verse closely, we become aware of the sign He is talking about—himself. Jonah was the sign to the people of Nineveh. It was not the miracles he did or the message he spoke, it was the fact that he came. He was the sign. This is why Jesus paralleled himself to Jonah.

In the final analysis, we are not dealing with church policy, rules, doctrines, or miracles. We have a literal person called Jesus with whom to deal.

Aside from doctrine or other people's opinions, we are confronted with the person of Christ. "What about Jesus? What position does He hold in my life?" We are called to embrace Him.

Prayer

"Jesus, thank You for Your example of walking on earth in victory and giving me the power that enables me to do the same."

• MATTHEW 12:38-42 •

Heb. 3:1

"Therefore, holy brothers, who share in the heavenly calling, fix your thoughts on Jesus, the apostle and high priest whom we confess."

PRIORITY REVIEW

Jesus is the only sign we will ever receive. Matthew tells us that He is "greater than the temple" (12:6).

If we consider the *position* of the Temple, we see it was the structure that was at the heart of all worship. Solomon had built the Temple. When it was dedicated, God descended and indwelt the structure. But Jesus is saying that He is greater than this structure. The Temple only contained a visitation from God, but Jesus was the actual person of God in their midst.

If we consider the *proclamation* of the Temple, we see that it was the law. Men were compelled to perform the ceremonies and offer the sacrifices according to the law of the Temple. But Jesus says that One greater than the law of the Temple was confronting them.

We also need to consider the *production* of the Temple. It soon became the heart of the religious life of the Jews. Pilgrimages were made to Jerusalem to visit the Temple.

We sometimes think more about the structures we build to represent God than the actual person of God. When that happens, the laws of the church become a higher value than the law of God.

Let's review our priorities lest we become temple-centered instead of Christ-centered.

Prayer

"Jesus, center my thoughts on You so that participation in Your earthly temple remains a means rather than an end."

MATTHEW 12:38-42

Matt. 12:42

"And now one greater than Solomon is here."

STANDING BEFORE US

The scribes and Pharisees demanded a sign from Jesus to prove His Messiahship. He answered, "And indeed a greater than Solomon is here" (Matt. 12:42).

In Solomon's *position* as king of Israel, he secured the kingdom. He prayed for wisdom, and God answered his prayer. Solomon wrote 3,000 proverbs and 1,005 songs. His wisdom was derived from God for the sake of judging Israel.

Solomon's *proclamation* was recorded in Ecclesiastes. He states that "all is vanity" except "fear God and keep His commandments" (12:8, 13).

The queen of Sheba traveled 1,200 miles to see Solomon's great *production*.

Jesus, the greater One, did not derive His wisdom from God. He said, "I *am* . . . the truth" (John 14:6). He was appointed by the Father to judge the whole of mankind.

Christ proclaims a pathway to the heart of God.

The One who is "greater than" stands before us, waiting for our acceptance.

Prayer

"Jesus, I accept You who have come from the Father for me."

• MATTHEW 12:38-42 •

1 Thess. 5:5, 8

"You are all sons of the light and sons of the day. . . . since we belong to the day, let us be self-controlled, putting on faith and love as a breastplate, and the hope of salvation as a helmet."

RESPONSE TO LIGHT

The scribes and Pharisees saw and heard more than they deserved, yet they still demanded a sign (Matt. 12:38). Jesus said to them, "The men of Nineveh will rise in the judgment with this generation and condemn it . . . The queen of the South will rise up in the judgment with this generation and condemn it" (vv. 41-42).

The people of Nineveh were Gentiles who were ignorant of God's Word until Jonah gave them his message. Upon hearing the truth, they received the light and repented. The queen of the South traveled 1,200 miles at great expense, hungering to know the truth and respond. This was in contrast to the Jews who were chosen by God from the beginning. They had revelation after revelation, yet they did not respond.

Does our degree of response match the amount of light we have received?

Prayer

"Jesus, grant me grace enough for this day to walk in the light I have received."

• MATTHEW 12:43-45 •

Ps. 127:1
"Unless the Lord builds the house, its builders labor in vain."

A HOUSE IN ORDER

In Matt. 12:43-45, Jesus tells the Pharisees the parable, an unclean spirit that had possessed them and spread throughout Israel. Under the leadership of John the Baptist, a revival was taking place, causing Israel's house to be swept clean and put in order. The unclean spirit roamed the dry places, looking for rest. He returned and possessed the empty house with seven other spirits worse than himself. Jesus states, "The last state of that man is worse than the first."

It is the story of one who sees truth and responds only partially. Disaster is inevitable for those who have developed the right actions and life-style but have never allowed their lives to be filled with the Holy Spirit. All goodness and righteousness accumulated is for naught without Him.

Prayer

"Jesus, build Your house in me. Fill me up with Your Spirit. Make my heart Your home."

• MATTHEW 12:43-45 •

1 John 1:9

"If we confess our sins, he is faithful and just and will forgive us our sins and purify us from all unrighteousness."

ABSENT, BUT NOT GONE

Jesus' powerful parable in Matt. 12:43-45 told of an unclean spirit that left a man and later returned to possess the same man with seven spirits worse than himself. This parable relates the truth that evil can be absent, but not gone.

Christ died to forgive and cleanse us from all unrighteousness (1 John 1:9). The power of sin can be broken, enabling a person to cease disobedience and begin to do what God wants him to do. Christ is the Enabler.

Not only can external sin deeds be cleansed, but internal sin can be cleansed as well. The carnal nature, which wars against God, can be crucified. Jesus died and rose from the dead to give each of us full and complete salvation. Rather than dealing with the *symptoms* of the sin disease, the internal *cause* can be healed. The cure is available for you.

Prayer

"Jesus, I want to live in the certainty of sins forgiven and a heart purified."

• MATTHEW 12:43-45 •

1 John 2:28
"And now, dear children, continue in him, so that when he appears we may be confident and unashamed before him at his coming."

MOMENT BY MOMENT

In addressing the scribes and the Pharisees, Jesus told a parable about them (Matt. 12:43-45). He was sharing the principle that evil can be absent, but not gone. It is true that sin can be absent, even removing its control through total deliverance. Evil may be absent; however, it is not gone. The evil one is a roaring lion, seeking to devour (1 Pet. 5:8). The battle may have been won, but the war is not over.

John Wesley often spoke of the moment-by-moment fellowship that we must have with Christ. Victory can only be maintained when we are constantly being filled with Him. Wesley said that if he was one moment without Christ, he was a devil again.

There are no "quick fixes" in this life, but we can have an intimate relationship with our Savior. He will be our constant victory.

Prayer
  "Jesus, thank You for the fellowship of relationship, which enables me to meet my life's moments with victory."

• MATTHEW 12:43-45 •

Phil. 1:9-11

"And this is my prayer: that your love may abound more and more in knowledge and depth of insight, so that you may be able to discern what is best and may be pure and blameless until the day of Christ, filled with the fruit of righteousness that comes through Jesus Christ—to the glory and praise of God."

EMPTY, BUT NOT FOR LONG

Jesus described the scribes and Pharisees as a house "empty, swept, and put in order" (Matt. 12:44).

The word Jesus used for empty has the connotation of being available because it is idle or unoccupied. The religious leaders could recite a long list of activities they did not participate in, but in the same breath they condemned everyone who did.

This negative spirit carries too far its pride in the things it doesn't do. While there may be some things the negative spirit legitimately wouldn't take part in, there seem to be many positive things left undone.

The negative heart is so busy condemning sin that it doesn't get around to loving the sinner. It talks loudly about the evil places teens go, but it never opens its home to ministry. While the hand is busy wagging a finger of condemnation, it cannot reach out to lift one in trouble. The mind is so filled with how bad things are that the heart cannot weep in intercessory prayer.

God, save us from a negative, empty spirit. May He instead fill the empty places with himself.

Prayer

"Jesus, keep me from a negative spirit by filling my inner being with Your presence."

• MATTHEW 12:43-45 •

Rom. 15:13
"May the God of hope fill you with all joy and peace as you trust in him, so that you may overflow with hope by the power of the Holy Spirit."

INTOLERABLE EMPTINESS

The truth is, no mind is truly idle. It is full of something. Life *will* be full; we choose what will fill it.

In Matt. 12:43-45, an unclean spirit left a man but returned with seven other spirits worse than himself. Jesus was right when He said, "The last state of that man is worse than the first."

To choose evil means that life will progress in sin. Stinginess in a young life will develop into greed. An unloving spirit soon turns into hate if tolerated.

The opposite is also true. Faith will grow into full-fledged belief. Love for Christ soon spreads to our fellowman.

We cannot be empty for long.

Prayer

"Jesus, my trust is in You to fill what could be intolerable emptiness with incomprehensible joy and peace."

• MATTHEW 12:46-50 •

1 Pet. 2:17

"Love the brotherhood of believers, fear God, honor the king."

RELATIONSHIP

An early martyr cried, "A Christian's only relatives are the saints." This parallels Jesus' reply when He was told that His mother and brothers were seeking Him.

He asked, "Who is My mother and who are My brothers?" He quickly answered His own question by pointing to His disciples and claiming them as His family. "For whoever does the will of My Father in heaven is My brother and sister and mother" (Matt. 12:46-50).

This introduces the great teachings of the seven parables spoken of in the 13th chapter. These parables tell us the mysteries of the kingdom of God, the heart of the mystery being that the kingdom of God is relationship.

The only thing that is eternal is relationship. The number one priority of our life should be our relationships.

Jesus wants a love relationship with each one of us. It is the reason He came: to establish a relationship with you.

Prayer

"Jesus, though it is difficult to comprehend Your love, I acknowledge and accept it with my obedience to Your will."

• MATTHEW 13:1-9 •

Eph. 5:1-2
"Be imitators of God, therefore, as dearly loved children and live a life of love, just as Christ loved us and gave himself up for us as a fragrant offering and sacrifice to God."

EXTRAVAGANT SOWING

In the parable of the sower, Matt. 13:4 talks about a *broad* falling of the seeds being sown.

A sower could take a bag of seed, walk through the field, and scatter handfuls at a time. He might also place a bag of seed on the back of a donkey, cut off a corner of the sack, and lead the donkey over the field. Either system of sowing has an element of carelessness about it. No one knew for sure where the seed was going. The wind might blow the seed up the road, into the gutter, or across the neighbor's field.

This type of "careless" sowing could better be described as extravagant. The Sower of the Word of God is like that. He extravagantly lavishes the Seed upon the world, holding nothing back in His attempt to reach this world with truth.

What a profound revelation to know that God has literally given all He has in order to draw us to himself. This extravagant sowing assures us of His love and enables us to participate in lavishing His love through us on our world.

Prayer

"Jesus, I pray for grace to extravagantly share Your love with those in and around the field in which I live, so that the love I have received spreads on up the road, finds the one in the gutter, and makes its way to my neighbor."

• MATTHEW 13:1-9 •

Matt. 13:9
"He who has ears, let him hear."

PERSONALLY YOURS

The gospel story is designed specifically for each one of us. Hundreds of people may hear it at the same time, but God deals with each one individually. In Matt. 13:9 it becomes apparent that the falling of the seed in the parable of the sower is a *personal* falling.

Jesus said, "He who has ears to hear, let him hear!" Jesus always comes back to our individual response. The multitudes of people are not His immediate concern, it is the individual. He alone has the ability to take the Seed of the Word and plant it specifically and personally in each heart.

What a privilege it is to be in His care and to receive His Word designed specifically for each one of us!

Prayer

"Jesus, I am listening with my ears and hearing with my heart. I respond to Your specific and personal sowing with my life."

• MATTHEW 13:1-9 •

John 12:36
"Put your trust in the light while you have it, so that you may become sons of light."

WHOLEHEARTED TRUST

"What is God's part and what is our part in relation to the matter of salvation?" Many cannot settle that issue, and the assurance of their salvation slips through their fingers.

Our obligation is a sincere heart and a willingness to do our part. But what is God's part? How far is He going to come in our direction?

In Matt. 13:1-9 Jesus convincingly tells us that He is the Sower who brings the Seed to our heart. God is adequate, and the Seed is fertile. We can rest in assurance that God is not going to leave us in limbo, because He is faithful.

Prayer

"Jesus, my trust is in You, for You have sown the Seed of truth and love in my heart. I rest in the assurance of Your faithfulness to nurture the Seed You have planted."

• MATTHEW 13:1-9 •

Phil. 1:6
"He who began a good work in you will carry it on to completion until the day of Christ Jesus."

NATURALLY

When we become aware that God has faithfully done His part on behalf of our salvation, it frees us to concentrate on our part.

What is our part in eternal salvation? There is a long list, ranging from church attendance, to singing in the choir, to consistent Bible study and prayer, to the giving of money. But what about when we do all of these things and still feel guilty, as though we could have done more?

In the parable of the sower (Matt. 13:1-9), Jesus pictures us as the soil whose obligation is to respond to the Seed that is planted. All Christ asks is an open response to His love.

Prayer

"Jesus, I have responded to Your love and have accepted the Seed of Your life. I accept my singular responsibility now to abide in You, the Vine, who alone can produce natural growth."

• MATTHEW 13:1-9 •

John 8:31-32

"Jesus said, 'If you hold to my teaching, you are really my disciples. Then you will know the truth, and the truth will set you free.'"

OPEN AND HONEST

Jesus tells us in Matt. 13:1-9 that we can come to Him just as we are. In fact, it is the only way we can come.

One does not have to fear an atheist if he is honest. Anyone who comes with an honest heart, searching for truth, will find God's personal revelation.

Many have habits that are difficult to break. These can be brought honestly to God, admitting need for His help. He will help in love.

God is approachable for those who come with open and honest hearts. This is the call to each of us from the parable of the sower.

Prayer

"Jesus, in openness and honesty, I lay out to You my life as it is. Shine the light of Your truth through me so that I can be free of defeat and live in Your victory."

• MATTHEW 13:1-9 •

Rev. 22:17
"'Come!' Whoever is thirsty, let him come; and whoever wishes, let him take the free gift of the water of life."

JUST AS YOU ARE

The parable of the sower shows us that we can come to Christ with an honest and open heart (Matt. 13:8).

This is illustrated by the story of a young lady who was raised in a Christian home but could not feel God's touch on her life. She sought a Christian experience in a variety of services, only to be disappointed.

One Sunday evening in a chapel, this young lady was confronted by an old-time preacher who pointed his finger right at her, saying, "You can be saved, just as you are." Heaven broke loose in her heart, and she found Christ that night.

Finding it impossible to sleep after receiving what she had long been seeking, Charlotte Elliott took pen and paper and began to write:

Just as I am, without one plea,
But that Thy blood was shed for me,
And that Thou bidd'st me come to Thee,
O Lamb of God, I come! I come!

We can come to Him just as we are. He delights in accepting us and making us His own.

Prayer

"Jesus, thank You for Your call, not to clean myself up before coming, but simply to come in honesty seeking You, just as I am."

• MATTHEW 13:10-17 •

1 John 3:1

"How great is the love the Father has lavished on us, that we should be called children of God!"

INVOLUNTARY ACTION

The disciples asked Jesus why He spoke in parables (Matt. 13:10). It is significant to note that Jesus began His answer with God's sovereignty (vv. 11-12).

In our humanistic society we tend to forget the sovereign God who is in charge. We have begun to think that we are dictating to the universe.

Even Christians sometimes develop a ho-hum attitude concerning the greatness of God. We believe that He will one day have the final word, and that He is certainly in charge of the universal decisions of the heavens; but my life is my business! God forgive us for such folly.

The message of the gospel is the story of God who has drawn so close that He has intimately tied himself to our daily life. He controls worlds, yet He is concerned for our individual world. The actions, plans, and needs of our lives do not escape His notice. Discovering this reveals the essence of life.

Prayer

"Jesus, in acknowledgment of Your loving and sovereign involvement in my life, I commit my life in service to You so that this love can be passed along, directing others back to You.

• MATTHEW 13:10-17 •

Matt. 11:27

"All things have been committed to me by my Father. No one knows the Son except the Father, and no one knows the Father except the Son and those to whom the Son chooses to reveal him."

MYSTERIES REVEALED

In Matt. 13:11-12 Jesus tells His disciples that God is sovereign in the law of revelation. You and I are incapable of knowing the beginning knowledge of the kingdom of God unless He decides to reveal it to us. Facts can be memorized, but the inward comprehension is impossible unless He intervenes.

Jesus uses words like "mysteries," which simply means "that which cannot be known unless it is revealed by someone." The King of the kingdom is sovereign in revealing these mysteries to us.

God has control over the truth, and He has the right to share it with us if He so desires. He is sovereign.

The good news is that Jesus does desire to share the truth with us. All we have to do is listen.

Prayer

"Jesus, as Your child I am available to listen to truth as You reveal it, and I am committed to walk in the light of truth revealed."

• MATTHEW 13:10-17 •

Matt. 11:29-30

"Take my yoke upon you and learn from me, for I am gentle and humble in heart, and you will find rest for your souls. For my yoke is easy and my burden is light."

LEAN ON ME

Because of His divine grace God has decided to reveal secrets about himself to us. What privileged people we are!

Matthew shares with us some of Jesus' insights into the sovereignty of God (Matt. 13:11-12). God is sovereign in the law of revelation (v. 11), and God is sovereign in the law of inertia (v. 12).

God wants man to be constantly growing spiritually. There should be no leaning back, resting on one level, or simply reveling in past achievements. In God's eyes we are either advancing or retreating in our spiritual journey.

When the disciples decided to follow Jesus, all they needed to grow in love, knowledge, and strength was to be theirs. What a promise! Guaranteed by God.

God wants to do the same for us. Right in the middle of the struggles of life, He has promised everything we need to advance spiritually. It is a promise we can lean on.

Prayer

"Jesus, thank You for the yoke of obedience, which brings rest from my struggle by giving the assurance of Your direction, so that I can grow and move forward."

• MATTHEW 13:10-17 •

Matt. 13:16

"But blessed are your eyes because they see, and your ears because they hear."

THE TRUTH OF RESPONSIBILITY

In Matt. 13:11-12, Jesus reminds the disciples of the sovereignty of God. This is a foundational cornerstone. However, there is an additional truth in verses 16-17 that must also be grasped: *man's responsibility.*

At first glance, these two truths may seem to be contradictory. If God is sovereign, man would be under His control and lose his ability to decide. Not so! We discover that the reason man is responsible is because God is sovereign.

In the Book of Matthew, every time the sovereignty of God is revealed, the responsibility of man is linked with that truth. God's sovereignty forms the basis for man to be accountable to Him.

This responsibility has long-range consequences in regard to life, family, and friends. We would be wise to investigate what is to be our responsibility.

Prayer

"Jesus, keep my eyes and ears open so that I see and hear clearly Your call and understand my responsibility to respond."

• MATTHEW 13:10-17 •

Ps. 27:1

"The Lord is my light and my salvation."

1 John 1:7

"If we walk in the light, as he is in the light, we have fellowship with one another, and the blood of Jesus, his Son, purifies us from all sin."

THE PRIVILEGE OF LIGHT

Jesus informs the disciples that they are responsible, because God is sovereign (Matt. 3:16-17). It is a responsibility we cannot shirk. Built into Jesus' accountability to the Father is our responsibility to the revelations of light given to us through the Son.

In studying Matthew 13, we realize that Matthew has not maintained proper chronological order in the events that have taken place. Jesus preaches a series of four parables in one setting to a great multitude. But, as Matthew records it, he places this personal gathering with His disciples in the middle of the sermon, immediately following the first parable.

The reason for this is that the truth of the parable of the sower has something to do with the answer to the disciples' question of Jesus' method of speaking in parables. As the soil is responsible for the seed placed within it, we, as disciples, are responsible for the revelation of truth implanted within us. God holds us accountable for the light of His revelation, stating that we will be judged according to the light we have received from Him.

Prayer

"Jesus, give me grace to live up to the privilege of light received, and the strength to continue walking in it even when I am distracted."

• MATTHEW 13:10-17 •

1 John 5:3-4
"This is love for God: to obey his commands. And his commands are not burdensome, for everyone born of God overcomes the world. This is the victory that has overcome the world, even our faith."

THE BLESSING OF OBEDIENCE

A strong biblical truth to keep in mind while studying the Book of Matthew is that of the free will of man. It is amazing to realize that a finite person can say no to an infinite God.

With this freedom comes personal responsibility. Jesus tells His disciples that we were *responsible for blessing.* "But blessed are your eyes for they see, and your ears for they hear" (Matt. 13:16).

The word "blessed" refers to divine grace. Jesus states that we have been favored by God. The mercies of God have been poured out upon us time after time. While others have been stumbling in darkness, we, His disciples, have received the light of God in full force.

As God invests His resource of grace in us, we become responsible for all the blessings of God that come our way.

Based upon these mercies and blessings, we are called to total surrender to Christ. In light of all God has done for us, we must accept our responsibility for living in the blessing of obedience.

Prayer

"Jesus, I want to live in total obedience to You. It is a blessing to be called, and a blessing to obey."

• MATTHEW 13:10-17 •

Col. 1:10-12

"And we pray this is order that you may live a life worthy of the Lord and may please him in every way: bearing fruit in every good work, growing in the knowledge of God, being strengthened with all power according to his glorious might so that you may have great endurance and patience, and joyfully giving thanks to the Father, who has qualified you to share in the inheritance of the saints in the kingdom of light."

HIGH, AND HOLY?

With privilege comes responsibility. In Matt. 13:17 Jesus called the disciples, saying, "For assuredly, I say to you that many prophets and righteous men desired to see what you see, and did not see it, and to hear what you hear, and did not hear it."

The Old Testament is full of stories of men who strained to grasp what you and I take for granted. We, too, often come to Sunday morning worship in a casual manner. The presence of the Holy Spirit is felt but makes little impact on us because we are so used to Him. But the prophets could not imagine a moment of such closeness to God. They would have given everything to be involved in a moment of time, experiencing the moving of the Holy Spirit.

We have been exposed to so much that we appreciate little. Have we accepted the responsibility of the knowledge and experience God has given us? We dare not take it for granted.

Prayer

"Jesus, because Your grace has given me so much, I want to live my life in gratitude for the privilege of sonship and the inheritance of the Kingdom."

• MATTHEW 13:10-17 •

Heb. 4:13
"Nothing in all creation is hidden from God's sight. Everything is uncovered and laid bare before the eyes of him to whom we must give account."

AN HONEST ACCOUNT

The natural outgrowth of God's sovereignty and man's responsibility is *judgment's inevitability*. Justice demands that a line be drawn. Man, who is responsible, must give an account.

There is no way to avoid God's judgment. It is a fact of life. It begins when we honestly seek God face-to-face. God has provided the means by which we can face His judgment now. It is judgment by grace, not wrath. It means alteration in our lives, but it is only for our good. The most difficult element contained in this judgment is honesty. We must allow God to probe all areas of our lives. In fact, we must invite it! Wait before Him! Listen!

Prayer

"Jesus, uncover everything in me so that my deepest thoughts lie bare before You. Reveal to me anything that needs purging so that I can stand before You and give an account, 'walking in all light received.'"

• MATTHEW 13:10-17 •

Rom. 5:17

"For if, by the trespass of the one man, death reigned through that one man, how much more will those who receive God's abundant provision of grace and of the gift of righteousness reign in life through the one man, Jesus Christ."

NOW

When we speak of judgment, we tend to think of the future. However, Jesus said to His disciples that there is a judgment taking place in our lives now (Matt. 13:13).

This is Jesus' answer as to why He speaks in parables. It has to do with God's judgment as a *divine hardening*. Jesus states that the Pharisees are hearing, but they have made the decision not to listen. They can see without any problem, but they have decided to ignore the truth of His Messiahship.

In fact, the Pharisees have progressed to the point of total rejection of Jesus. In chapter 12 they band together to plot the murder of Christ. So Jesus preaches to them in parables, which is a form of hiding the truth of God. The parables are a form of judgment to those who have rejected.

There is a definite penalty to pay, even now, for rejecting the truth. Each time we refuse to listen, a hardening process takes place in the heart. The ability to refuse Christ now increases the ability to refuse Him later. The time for acceptance is now.

Prayer

"Jesus, keep me open, my heart flexible and willing, so that from the day of acceptance of Your abundant provision of grace I continue to grow and increase in the ability to discern Your voice above all others."

• MATTHEW 13:18-23 •

2 Tim. 2:22

"Flee the evil desires of youth, and pursue righteousness, faith, love and peace."

THE DETERMINING FACTOR

In the parable of the sower, Jesus tells us that the seed represents the Word of the Kingdom (Matt. 13:19). It is the living, energetic, life-changing power of the Word of God that comes to our heart that is able to do all that is necessary as we respond.

Jesus also shows us that He is the Sower. The Seed and the Sower are not on trial. They are both adequate for the task of changing life. It is the soil that stands to be judged.

Jesus tells us that the soil is the heart, our real, inner being; the very source of life itself. The heart, the center point of life that is the seat of affection, is what motivates and determines life.

It is how we respond to the Word in our heart that determines our entire life. The condition of the heart is our greatest concern.

Prayer

"Jesus, I respond from my heart to the seeds of the truth of eternal life, so that growth may be produced in righteousness, faith, love, and peace."

• MATTHEW 13:18-23

Lev. 11:44

"I am the Lord your God; consecrate yourselves and be holy, because I am holy."

HANNAH

Our response to the gospel depends on the condition of our hearts. In the parable of the sower Jesus gives us some examples.

He begins with the soil, which in this case is the pathway (Matt. 13:19). We'll call this soil "Hard-hearted Hannah."

"Hannah" is tougher than nails and lets everyone know it. We never have to guess what she is thinking or where she stands on any issue. Her pathway has been trodden by the busy feet of a thousand activities. Although these activities are not bad in themselves, Hannah has been lured into the busy patterns of legitimate living and has been beaten into hardness. As a matter of survival, activities have squeezed out the presence of Christ.

Prayer

"Jesus, help me look clearly at the activities of my life to make sure that in my busyness to serve, I have not hardened my ears to hear."

• MATTHEW 13:18-23 •

Prov. 19:23

"The fear of the Lord leads to life."

CORRECT RESPONSE

"Hard-hearted Hannah" is the name we have given to the hardened pathway in the parable of the sower (Matt. 13:19). Her condition: hardness due to the busyness of activities. The cause: Satan, who pressures us with evil temptation and with the daily distractions of life, which undermine our priority system.

Most of us feel we have been trapped in a pressured schedule, but it is not true. Everything in which we are involved has come as a direct result of our own choice. We do what we want to do. Our schedule is not out of control unless we let it be.

We need to correct, then, our response to Jesus as Lord of our life. With Him to guide, we can begin to make the adjustments. In fact, He is the only chance for hope of correction. In our own strength we are unable to adjust under the pressures, even if we clearly see the need. Jesus alone can keep our heart from becoming hard.

Prayer

"Jesus, keep me from becoming 'Hard-hearted Hannah' as I respond to my need for Your Lordship in my life."

• MATTHEW 13:18-23 •

Jer. 17:8

"He will be like a tree planted by the water that sends out its roots by the stream. It does not fear when heat comes; its leaves are always green. It has no worries in a year of drought and never fails to bear fruit."

DEEPLY PLANTED

The second soil Jesus describes in the parable of the sower is the "stony places" (Matt. 13:20-21). From His description we have designed the name "Shallow, Hollow Holly."

I don't like "Shallow, Hollow Holly" at all. She is so deceptive. She has the same condition as "Hard-hearted Hannah" except she keeps it hidden. By placing a layer of dirt over the top of her hard heart, she deceives those with whom she comes in contact.

Holly's chief characteristic is impulsiveness (v. 20). She attempts to live the Christian life on emotion. In special services down at the church, she responds with emotional enthusiasm that only lasts about two weeks. During a special project, she really gets involved, but this enthusiasm only lasts for a few days. Holly's life is governed by her emotional feelings at the moment, rather than a committed life-style of service regardless of how she feels.

Jesus wants the roots of our commitment to go deeper than emotions. He calls us to a deep, total commitment of our innermost being.

Prayer

"Jesus, I hear Your deep, internal heartbeat, which calls me to a deep and total commitment. Scrape off any layers of dirt I have used to deceive myself. Plant my total being deep in You."

• MATTHEW 13:18-23 •

Jer. 17:9-10, 14

"The heart is deceitful above all things and beyond cure. Who can understand it? 'I the Lord search the heart and examine the mind.' ...

"Heal me, O Lord, and I will be healed; save me and I will be saved, for you are the one I praise."

MORE THAN THE MOMENT

"Shallow, Hollow Holly" is described by Jesus as the stony places (Matt. 13:20-21), responding with shallow emotions without a deep commitment.

What causes such a condition? The cause is complex. We cannot limit the blame to the world, although the world is part of the cause. The advertisements of the world have put an emotional bottle into our mouths, and we have drained it dry, too often becoming emotional buyers dangling at the end of its string.

But the church has often been guilty of the same, appealing to the emotional level of people until Christianity sometimes becomes a feeling rather than a life-changing commitment.

Our emotions can lead us astray. We must not let how we feel at any particular moment be the determining factor of our lives. God is bigger than our emotions. We must make a commitment to Him that goes to the heart of our lives. He is worthy of our total being.

Prayer

"Jesus, beyond the emotions of the moment I recommit my life to You day by day so that my commitment to You is at the heart of my life and not the surface of my feelings."

• MATTHEW 13:18-23 •

2 Chron. 16:9

"For the eyes of the Lord range throughout the earth to strengthen those whose hearts are fully committed to him."

CLEARING THE CLOUDS

"Shallow, Hollow Holly," the second soil in the parable of the sower (Matt. 13:20-21), stands in need of correction. She lives on an emotional level, encouraged by her environment. The answer for her predicament is found at the end of the parable.

Jesus says, "He who has ears to hear, let him hear!" (v. 9). Jesus urges us to grasp with our mind the great need for commitment to Him, which goes beyond our level of feeling. Christ must become Lord of our hearts (the center of our lives), not just for a moment of feeling.

Our emotions may play tricks on us and leave us unable to see the reality of situations. Only the strong eyes of faith that are stimulated by the commitment of total surrender to His Lordship can carry us through.

God doesn't want us to react only emotionally to His call. He seeks our surrender from the deepest level of our being. What will we do?

Prayer

"Jesus, clear the clouds of emotions around my life so that I can be sure of a full and deep surrender to You."

• MATTHEW 13:18-23 •

Col. 3:2, 15

"Set your minds on things above, not on earthly things. . . . [and] Let the peace of Christ rule in your hearts, since as members of one body you were called to peace."

VALUE CENTER

In Matt. 13:22, some of the seeds fell on the thorn-infested soil. When good seed is planted in this soil, it may produce growth, but the life is soon choked by the thorns. In this parable the thorns represent "the cares of this world and the deceitfulness of riches."

We'll name this soil "Fickle, Freckled Frederick," for Frederick is an individual whose materialistic environment has engulfed his life. The word "choke" is used in the story of 2,000 pigs rushing into the sea and drowning. The word for "choked" and "drowned" is the same (Mark 5:13; Luke 8:33). It is a picture of being overcome with, submerged in, and dominated by.

In our materialistic society things may grip our lives until we are dominated by materialism. We allow possessions to set our standards, determine our values, and control our attitudes.

Christ can bring freedom from a materialistic lifestyle. Our value system moves away from temporary things to become centered on an eternal quality of life.

Prayer

"Jesus, free me from the allure of temporary materialism by focusing my thoughts on You and Your call to an eternal quality of life."

• MATTHEW 13:18-23 •

Isa. 35:8-10

"And a highway will be there; it will be called the Way of Holiness. The unclean will not journey on it; it will be for those who walk in that Way . . . only the redeemed will walk there . . . Gladness and joy will overtake them, and sorrow and sighing will flee away."

ETERNALLY REAL

There is a rampant disease that is in the process of devouring the souls of this generation. It has to do with living in an illusionary world, where so much time is spent living in make-believe that the unreal becomes real.

Jesus uses "Fickle, Freckled Frederick," our name for the third soil in the parable of the sower, to teach us that "the deceitfulness of riches choke the word, and he becomes unfruitful" (Matt. 13:22).

Jesus speaks of the illusion of riches. We can stockpile riches and rest our security upon them as a foundation, but eventually we will discover the lie. There is no security to be found in materialism. One can brag of land ownership, but 100 years from now it will not be ours. Ownership is an illusion; it is not secure.

Our ultimate security is in eternal things. "Jesus Christ is the same yesterday, today, and forever" (Heb. 13:8). We can trust Him! He is eternally real.

Prayer

"Jesus, direct me in the real path of holiness, away from the illusion of riches, toward the richness of eternal joy."